Finding Love and Purpose: Our Journey to Healing through Connection

Sarina Baptista, Vickie Hays,
Carrie Hackwelder-Longo, and Kimberly Latta

Copyright © 2023 Sarina Baptista, Vickie Hays, Carrie Hackwelder-Longo, and Kimberly Latta

Bridge to Healing Press 2023
Edited by Claire Shepherd, Shepherd Editing

All rights reserved. No part of this book may be used or reproduced by any means, graphic, electronic, or mechanical, including photocopying, recording, taping or by any information storage retrieval system without the written permission of the publisher except in the case of brief quotations embodied in critical articles and reviews.

ISBN: 978-0-9912552-3-8 (sc)

Because of the dynamic nature of the internet, any web addresses or links contained in this book may have changed since publication and may no longer be valid.

The authors of this book do not dispense medical advice or prescribe the use of any technique as a form of treatment for physical, emotional, or medical problems without the advice of a physician, either directly or indirectly. The intent of the authors is only to offer information of a general nature to help you in your quest for emotional and spiritual wellbeing. In the event you use any of the information in this book for yourself, which is your constitutional right, the authors and the publisher assume no responsibility for your actions.

Printed in the United States of America
Cover design by Sarina Baptista
Images by Bruno, GDJ and JuliusH via Pixabay
Interior book design by BEAUTeBOOK
Bridge to Healing Press First Edition August 13, 2023

*This book is dedicated to all who are seeking love and purpose.
May your loved ones guide you to beautiful discoveries!*

TABLE OF CONTENTS

Introduction	i
Chapter One: The Beginning	1
Chapter Two: Mediums By Chance	15
Chapter Three: Together Again	29
Chapter Four: Healing and Growth	43
Chapter Five: Now	55
Epilogue: In Their Own Words	67
Postscript: Writing This Book	79
Acknowledgments	83
About The Authors	84
Resources	87

Introduction

To introduce this book, we must introduce all of the authors and contributors. This book was written by four women, all of whom experienced huge loss and grief in very traumatic ways. Each of these women found that their grief experience was a bit different than the norm. What set these women apart was not just their methods of grief, but also their quest for answers.

Why did my loved one leave?
Where did my loved one go?
Is this all there is?
Is my loved one out there somewhere waiting for me?
Is my loved one trying to communicate with me?
Will I ever see my loved one again?
How do I continue my life without my loved one here?

Each of these women sought actual answers to these questions and did so by bypassing "normal" sources of information. But, then again, none of our authors have ever been "normal." Each has had their own spiritual encounters and awakenings throughout the years. With certainty, though, this awakening, beyond any doubt, became much more than just a quest to find answers about their loved ones' passing and where they are now. This awakening became a launching point, the beginning of a new journey, one beyond the comprehension of our finite world and its workings.

To say that these women were meant to meet and bond in this way would be an understatement. All of these women now understand their meeting and working together was in the plan all along. But, whose plan?

It's time to introduce the contributors of this book. These co-authors are the reason this book exists. They are also the reason these women met.

Justin. Justin was a high school junior when he felt called to action following the attacks of September 11, 2001. When discussing his decision to later enlist in the US Marine Corps with his parents, he explained that he could not "stand by while others fight for our freedom." His charisma, integrity, and laser-focused determination touched the lives of many. Justin was killed in action at the age of 26.

Chase. Chase was a gentle giant who stood up for the underdog and guided broken souls to seek help. He was also a musician who wrote, produced, and played each part in an album he finished just days before he passed. This album can be found under the title *Unexamined* by Chase Longo with Top Floor Records on SoundCloud. Chase was 21 years old when he passed.

Dan. Despite facing many challenges throughout his life, Dan dedicated himself to learning and living an intentional, purposeful, and generous life. He enjoyed sharing his gifts and skills to support others and celebrating life's special moments.

J.T. J.T. was seven years old when he passed. At his funeral, child after child stood to say he was their best friend, and how he helped them through something, whether it was being sad at school, or sharing his treat, or just saying "I'm here." At seven years old, he had compassion and wisdom that he shared with everyone he met.

This book exists because of the incredible, unconditional love of these four souls. If not for their determination, persistence, and tenacity, we would not have these stories to tell. They are the true authors and motivators for this work. As you will read, each of these co-authors wanted more for their loved ones here. They all wanted to answer those questions: Why? Where? When? How? And the way in which they connected and communicated with our authors is proof—proof that those who leave us are never truly gone. It is their job to help us through our grief, to do everything they can to help us navigate the "new norm" here without them. And, for these very patient contributors, it is also to help us discover that love never truly dies. Each of us has a very special purpose to bring forward to others—to share our stories, to help others understand that this connection is not only real, but it is attainable. Yes, connection with the other side is attainable. Our four authors can attest to that.

This book is also designed to help you, the reader, connect with the other side. As you read, be observant of the energy around you. Your loved ones who have passed will never scare you or come with judgment. They have unbounded love for you. We hope you will be open to receive from them just as you receive from this book's authors and contributors.

Chapter One
The Beginning

Vickie

"The State Police are looking for you." It was my husband, Steve, calling. I was unloading the car and stopped to catch my breath before making what felt like the hundredth trip up the stairs to my second story condo.

"Why?" was all I managed to get out, puzzled, my mind racing with possibilities. Was there an accident? Is it one of the kids? I mentally ran through everyone's schedules: Adrienne, Matt and the kids were home; Morgan was at her nanny job; and Veronica was in a boat on a lake fishing with a friend. I had just texted Veronica, though, so I knew all was okay with her. Justin, of course, was deployed. And I had watched enough movies to know that if something had happened to Justin, the Marine Corps would deliver the news, not the State Police.

"I don't know; they wouldn't tell me. But I have a number that you're supposed to call." We ended the conversation so I could finish my last trip from the car to the condo and return the phone call. Just inside the door, my phone rang again. On the other end was a man that identified himself as a detective with the Michigan State Police. The detective asked if I could come to the station. When I explained that I was an hour away, he quickly stated that he would come to me. He still did not say why, but I could expect someone soon. There was something about his voice, something that made me think he wasn't telling me everything. "Are my kids okay?" I asked. The detective gave me a generic, unconvincing response, and I instinctively knew that something was very wrong. "How soon can I expect you?" I asked. The detective responded that it would be two to three hours. By now I was convinced that something was very wrong and offered to drive to the station. I reminded him that I could be there in an hour. He again assured me that someone would be by very soon.

I opened my laptop, trying to distract myself while I waited. What if one of the girls is in trouble with the law? What could the State Police possibly want to discuss with me? Over and over and over again, I contemplated the possibilities of why the State Police would want to talk to me. A few minutes later, there was a knock at my door. I hopped up to open the door, expecting it to be a neighbor stopping by to say hello. Instead, I was shocked to see two uniformed Marine Corps officers. My heart sank, instantly knowing the reason for their visit. I immediately spun around and walked away, leaving the door open. "No! No! This can't possibly be happening," I screamed silently in my head. "Please, don't say it!"

I turned around, and the officers were still standing outside my door, looking very uncomfortable. I found myself feeling sorry for them. How terrible it must be, to be the one to tell someone like me of a loss this incredible. I asked them both to come in and closed the door behind them. I sat down, putting on my best brave face, and one began to talk. He introduced himself and his companion and then told me that Justin had been killed in action at 8:00 am in Helmad Province, Afghanistan.

He kept talking, but I couldn't hear him. I went over the events of the day in my mind, recalling that "feeling" I always had when Justin was going to call. I had purposely kept my cell phone nearby so that I wouldn't miss his call. There had been several missed calls over the past few months—never by much, just a minute or two, or by simply not reaching the phone before that last ring. The missed calls would leave me anxiously waiting until Justin was able to try again, as there was not a way for me to call him. It had been frustrating for both of us. I was sure he would call me; why hadn't he called me? This must be a mistake. Could this really be happening?

The Beginning

I asked the two Marine officers to leave so that I could notify my family. I was not sure how this all played out but, now that I had been notified, I knew that the news of our loss would be released to the media. I didn't want Justin's sisters, my parents, or my siblings to learn any of this on the news, and I felt I was racing the clock. I spoke with my brother and attempted to contact my sister. I drove to my daughter Adrienne's home. From there, I made the 30-minute drive to my parent's house and then headed back home to meet with my daughters, Morgan and Veronica. Sometime along the drive, I was able to reach my sister's husband and make a call to my boss. So much love, so many tears, and such disbelief. So much pain.

The next hours and days are a blur. We traveled to Dover Air Force Base to meet Justin on his arrival back to US soil and then began to plan his funeral. Many of his military "brothers"—those with whom Justin had served—were traveling from around the world to attend his service, and my attention turned to taking care of them. Our friends graciously arranged accommodations, transportation, and food for approximately 35 Marines. They began to arrive a few days prior to the service, and we spent that time getting to know one another. Having an opportunity to share our stories of Justin with these men, and they with us—merging Justin's personal and military life—formed a bond that we will share forever.

Justin's service was nothing shy of spectacular. It was held in the gymnasium of his high school, and it was filled. A line of people ran the entire length of the gymnasium, out the door and down the hallway, all waiting to pay their respects. I stood at Justin's side, holding his hand, and thanked each one. The amount of community and military support was astounding, and his service was an accurate, heartfelt expression of love for this incredible man, for my son. The service ended at the cemetery. The sky was a beautiful blue, without a single cloud, and even nature seemed to stand still to honor Justin. At the conclusion, the minister gave the final prayer. As he said the final "Amen," a loud clap of thunder rumbled on this beautiful, clear-blue sky day. My boy was home.

The guests returned to their homes and families. I returned to work, and we all tried to move forward. Everyone assured me that time would heal; I was less than convinced.

My blur continued for months. Following his funeral, I attended many wonderful events honoring Justin. His high school football team retired his jersey (No #54) with a home game entitled "Hansen Night." The Marine Corps held a celebration of life a few months later, after his team returned from Afghanistan. I tried, and felt I was failing miserably, to help my girls, my family, and Justin's friends make sense of this loss. All the while, I kept thinking, *Is he really gone? Why do I feel him? If he were gone, wouldn't I feel his absence?* I even talked with him in my mind. In those conversations, Justin would assure me that everything would be okay, that everything had changed and would never be the same, but that we would all be okay.

I continued going through the motions, trying to make sense of things, trying desperately to find that space where I could breathe. How would I face the rest of my life without my son? I knew how to research and find answers. What I was unable to find was the answer to how to address the grief I was feeling, this incredible, breathtaking pain that was so overwhelming and all-encompassing. There was no visible solution, only despair. How would I face the rest of my life without my son? How does anyone do that? And why don't I feel his absence? What kind of mother would not feel her son's absence when he was clearly gone?

Carrie

It was the day my mother received her cancer diagnosis that I had my first meaningful connection with Spirit. At the time, I had no idea what was going on. Now I realize that it was guidance that I would desperately need—and continue to need—as I would lose my mother within months. And just over four years later, I would lose my son. Without that glimpse into what comes next, I don't know if I would have been capable of surviving any of this loss. Connection with Spirit and confirmation that love lives on is how I've been able to cope and keep moving forward.

As it was, that day was due to be a difficult day because we were headed to the viewing of a family friend, Mary Alice, who had passed away after a long battle with emphysema. Our family is deeply intertwined with Mary Alice's, so we were already very somber and quiet that morning. My son, daughter, and I would be making the hour-and-a-half trip to Pittsburgh to attend the visitation. My mother would be missing it because of an appointment she had for a mass they had found in her chest which had been causing her pain for months. Mary Alice was one of my mother's closest friends, so her absence from the viewing felt heavy and foreboding. Mom and I were inseparable, so it would be unusual to attend such a serious family function without her. There was no escaping the grief and gravity of the day's coming events.

That same morning, my son, Chase, had a basketball tournament in St. Mary's which was about an hour in the opposite direction. He headed that way with a teammate, and I would be picking him up midday and making the trip to Pittsburgh. So, I spent the morning with the intention of just going through the motions of preparing myself mentally for all that was going to happen that day. I was moving about quietly doing dishes and household chores. While doing so, my paternal grandmother who had been gone for more than twenty years "popped" into my head. I could see her head and shoulders and she was smiling this amazing smile. She looked so vibrant and full of joy. I saw her as the image of a very vivid dream that remains in your mind all day. She was not outside of my vision, but at the front of it in my mind. She was bathed in what looked to be the most incredible white light that radiated peace and love. I could see the sunny day and trees behind her, and this beautiful light pouring down around her. She didn't say anything; I just had this vision of her, and it lasted for what seemed like hours. She was with me when I did the dishes, while I swept, while I folded laundry. In my mind, I asked my grandmother, "What is this about? Mary A.?" The two were best friends. Was she here for her? I intuitively knew that it wasn't for her. I was beginning to get unnerved. I continued to get ready for the day. I was in the shower, and she was still with me. Finally, I asked her if this was about my mom. Suddenly, I had this series of relatives flip through my mental vision like a slideshow, all vibrant and full of joy, and bathed in that same light—my grandfather, Great-Uncle Bob, Great-Uncle Danny, Mrs. Murray, and Mary Alice. I knew at that moment that my mother was not going to survive this illness. I also knew that my family was showing me that love lives on, and that my mom would be okay. Well, not just okay, but happy and surrounded by loved ones and bathed in love and light. Her pain would be gone, and she would be at peace.

I didn't take it well, though. I was full of grief and heartbroken at the prospect of losing my mom. She and I were so incredibly close. I couldn't imagine my life without her. And, simply put, I wasn't ready to lose her. I asked my visions to leave. After years of meditating, visiting mediums, praying, and working to get messages, I finally "got" something, and I was asking them to leave! I was so upset. Once I realized that they were trying to help, I called a friend who also was able to receive from Spirit, and I asked her if this experience sounded familiar and if the spirits would be offended that I told them to go. I was a mess and torn between appreciating how awesome this experience was and how distraught I was at the thought of losing my mom. My friend assured me that the message was not meant to be upsetting, and if I needed to be alone for a time, they would understand. On our drive from St. Mary's to Pittsburgh, my mother called me to tell me she received a diagnosis of stage four lung cancer. Within five months, my mother was gone.

After getting that message, I received a few more visits from Spirit while my mom was sick. Friends of ours who passed "popped in" on my drive to see my mom in the hospital—always in that beautiful light looking whole, happy, and well. My maternal grandmother "popped" in while I was teaching kindergarten, letting me know how proud she was of me because I was a teacher. At that point, I had no real control over the visits. I did learn that grief complicates the ease with which I can connect at times.

Even though Spirit showed me that they are happy on the other side, I grieved my mother so deeply. For three years, the heavy loss of my mother weighed on me. I couldn't reach her. When I tried to quiet myself and meditate, I could literally envision a mass of black scribbles in my mind, all chaos and negativity. I was frustrated. Before she passed, she promised to do what she could to reach me. In all, it took about three years for me to let go of my grief and get out of my own way. I kept meditating and pushing through the break in my meditation where I would begin to cry. Eventually, I was able to see her in my meditations. We wouldn't communicate, but she was there, and she was happy and well. I was on my way to her.

Kim

As I sat in the hospice room for the last time, I could never have imagined the journey that was about to unfold for me. I was so "in the moment," listening for sounds that my husband, Dan, needed my help and touching him, maybe for the last time. I could not see the beginning of what was ahead. I could only see the ending to our time together. I couldn't imagine something different, let alone something better, for both of us. I watched the end of his weak, limiting body, and felt unending guilt about not doing enough to make his life the best it could be while trying to help support us with my demanding job fifty miles away. The last two days of Dan's life had a shocking urgency, yet we moved through them with an efficiency and closeness that, to date, I had never experienced. And as hard as it was, I left the choice of care up to him. It was less than twenty-four hours from the time Dan refused to be intubated for a second time and agreed to move to hospice, to the time we said goodbye. Before our time together ended, I played him our favorite song, "Harvest Moon." We would dance to this song in our living room each fall. And in this moment, it made him smile. I said all of the "I love yous" I had thought about saying over the years but didn't always say out loud. The last night we spent together seemed as natural and normal as it could be with me getting the nurse to suction his throat every few hours so that he could continue to breathe. We gathered in a circle around him, holding hands, just me and the hospice staff. They would later describe Dan's passing as the most peaceful death they had ever witnessed.

As peaceful as the last few moments of Dan's life were, I was numb for the next few months. Returning to work felt almost impossible. Because of COVID, all employees were told to work from home and the only office space in our house was Dan's. I remember sitting in his office, surrounded by his things, unable to move. I resented the imposition of work on our personal space, on our home. I have always been such an independent person, so it was shocking to me that I was having such trouble standing on my own, suddenly losing the will to go on by myself. I was frozen in time, trying to find the motivation to move forward—anywhere. I couldn't go back to the way things were, but I couldn't seem to go forward either. I wondered when or how I would ever start caring about my life again. I quit my job because I literally couldn't make myself do it. I became stuck in Dan's favorite room of our house, our guest room. We used to laugh as our giant master bedroom sat empty and we snuggled ourselves and our two dogs into the tiny bedroom. Something about its size encouraged us to cuddle up and made us feel safe. We watched television, read books to each other, and talked before going to sleep. We celebrated a belated Christmas due to Dan's first hospital stay and opened our presents to each other on that bed less than a month before Dan passed. Our whole life was wrapped up in that tiny guest room. And because of that, I couldn't leave it.

Ironically, it was Dan who, unknowingly at the time, led me to the second psychic medium I had ever met. Sarina Baptista, a local medium, was doing a talk at our library about a book she had written after the loss of her son. Dan was always interested in learning new things, and he invited me to go hear her speak. Something changed in me that night, but not so much for him. I tease him about that now. He wasn't nearly as interested as I was in the topic of communicating with our loved ones who had passed. I was the one who followed up with Sarina to be sure the loved ones I had lost most recently were "doing okay." It was incredibly comforting to check in with each of my parents and a pet I had recently lost under difficult circumstances. Each connection took on the personality of the physical being I had known. It was heart-wrenching at the time, but I was reassured that I had allowed each of them to go when it was the right time. Although I was there to check in with certain souls, others showed up, including all of the dogs I had the pleasure of living with over the years. No one had left me. They were all still there, waiting to help. I know now that this is what prepared me for what was to come.

I contacted Sarina soon after Dan's passing. I needed to know he was okay, but initially, I was not ready for his help or his advice. Early on, Sarina described it as a veil of grief that clouded my ability to hear or easily accept the messages. That veil persisted for almost a year but dissolved more with each passing day. Dan was such a serious man, and he let very few people see the silly, child-like side of him that almost immediately started emerging during my sessions with Sarina. Now that he had been freed from the psychological pain of his childhood and years of illness after his life was "saved" from stage 4 cancer, he was almost giddy. His glee was so powerful that Sarina snickered through his messages, which added levity and comfort to a very dark time for me. Dan always "showed up" well before Sarina was done with her introduction and invitation and would cut her short, ready to get on with it – eager to help me. I remember him saying "I'm sorry I left you but now you are free to do the things you are meant to do." At the time I didn't understand what that meant, but the message continues to ring truer with each passing day. I couldn't have quit my job and started down this path if he was still alive. I was a caretaker of and partner to a very sick man for the majority of our lives together, and I had no time to hear or follow my new calling. But now that I can embrace my new path, and know that he supports me, I can't imagine living my life any other way. I know people say that he is in a better place, and he is. He really is.

One of the first messages Dan shared with me (through Sarina) was that it was no one's fault that he had passed—not the hospital and not the doctors. He knew I was asking the question "why" things had gone so badly so quickly, and if the doctors, who seemed baffled at the time, could have done something to save his life. He said they didn't understand what they were dealing with yet. His body was very frail from the harsh cancer treatment he had endured years ago, but his breathing was not a serious problem. Then suddenly, for no reason that they understood, his ability to breathe failed quickly, and in less than twenty-four hours, he was gone. Less than a month later, COVID was in the news. Dan says he hears me talking to him (which I do a lot—usually out loud), and he says he is talking back. I don't necessarily hear him respond, but I end up just knowing things that had to have come from him. I also know now that he gives me suggestions and direction often. But, before I could recognize the new role that he would play in my life, I had to believe that there would be better times ahead for me. And there were incredible moments and days mixed in with the incredible sadness. And my husband, from an unbelievable place, helped me out of the hole of grief and showed me what was possible. He wasn't gone. He was still there, ready to help whenever I needed it. I just had to believe…and to ask. Little did I know, this was just the beginning.

Sarina

I was a stay-at-home mom with my three beautiful children, J.T., Alessia, and Anthony. We moved to Colorado in 2005 when the kids were five, three, and one, respectively. Our neighborhood was one of those amazing places where everyone knew one another, and there was always someone around if you needed anything. In March 2007, my family and I found that we definitely needed help, the kind of help you couldn't ever dream of needing.

It was a Friday, March 30th. J.T. and Alessia caught the flu earlier in the week, so I was focused on taking care of them, making sure they were comfortable. After all, it was just the flu. My daughter had a fever and was not keeping food down, so I hopped between her room and J.T.'s to see what they needed. Thursday, March 29th, I got food poisoning. I was feverish, achy, and had major intestinal cramping. My fever broke finally at 11 p.m. that night, and I felt almost human. I was still very weak, but knew my babies needed me, so I checked on both of them to see how they were feeling. My daughter was already asleep, but J.T. was very restless. We went for a drive around the neighborhood to see if that would help. It was a temporary fix. When we returned, we decided to hang out in his room for a bit. By this time, it was about 3 a.m. I figured since I was sick all day, I needed to spend time with my boy. He didn't seem tired, and again, was agitated. He did sleep for maybe a half hour. I was resting in the bed next to him, and just about asleep when he popped up in his bed and said, "Mom, go to your room." I said, "What? You want to go to the big bed to try to rest in there?" I was thinking maybe he wanted to go to sleep on the master bed for more room and a change of scenery. He said, "No, you go. I want to watch TV." J.T. knew I couldn't sleep with the TV on, so it made sense to me at the time for him to send me out of the room. Later, looking back, this was very out of character. He loved being with his mama, so sending me out of the room was not something he would do. Of course, I was exhausted from the day, not thinking clearly.

I said, "Okay, you watch TV and try to get some rest. I'll be back to check on you. I love you, bud." He said, "I love you, Mom," and I left the room. I went to my bedroom and climbed into bed. I was so exhausted from being sick all day, and then caring for two sick children, so I was out like a light.

At 6 a.m. I awoke, just two hours later. I headed to J.T.'s room to check on him, and something stopped me. A thought came into my head, *What if he's not alive? Oh my God. Knock that off!* I passed it off as a lack of sleep and continued across the hall. I looked in, and he looked so peaceful. Until I saw his chest wasn't moving. I screamed for my husband, who got him off the bed and I started CPR. My husband called 911, and before I knew it, the police, fire, and EMS were all trying to get my J.T. to come back. I knew he wasn't coming back, though. I knew when I started

CPR. I kept praying, though, screaming at him to get back into his body and to not leave me.

Forty-five minutes later, he was ambulanced to the hospital. I didn't even realize the ambulance had left with him. I threw on some clothes and remember asking the fireman and police officer what his chances were. Their faces were very grim. The officer tried to give me some hope. He said, "Well, he was still a little warm."

My husband, John, had to stay with Alessia and Anthony until we could find someone to watch them, so I drove to the hospital on my own. I called my dear friend, Jen, who I knew was intuitive. At the time, I had no idea I had these gifts also. She told me to tell him to get back into his body, to not leave. She said, "Yell at him! Scream! Tell him he has to do this!" Both of us sensed this wasn't going to happen, but I kept pleading and screaming, hoping my commands would work, and I would get my boy back.

When I arrived at the hospital, they whisked me into a little room next to the emergency room lobby. I didn't know why, other than they didn't want me to cause a scene, maybe? I learned later this is the room where they take you when they know your loved one isn't going to make it. I was met by a beautiful nurse, my angel, Paula. She held my hand as we waited for the doctors. An hour later, the doctor came in, sat down, and said, "We lost him." My husband hadn't arrived yet, and I didn't know what to do. I called him and asked if he had someone to watch the kids, and more importantly, someone to drive him to the hospital. The police chaplain offered to do this. The words came out of my mouth, words I never, ever thought I would have to say to my husband. "J.T. didn't make it."

I'd like to say I awoke the following day knowing exactly what happened to my beautiful boy, but that was not the case. It would be weeks until we received the coroner's report citing "Complications due to Influenza A." After an extensive call with the medical examiner, he said J.T. had scarring in his lungs, most likely due to his premature birth at 36 weeks. I would later learn this was all a setup, a plan to which we all agreed. It was the cosmic kick in the ass to get me to work on my true purpose: the bridge between this world and the next.

Chapter Two
Mediums by Chance

Vickie

A few days after Justin's funeral, I stopped by to visit his grave. Morgan happened to be there with a few others, and it was my first opportunity to see her since the funeral. She told me, "That's so cool, Mom, that you got Justin site #54." What? I had? Confused, I looked around and Morgan pointed out the marker and, in plain sight, was a round, flat marker with #54!

Justin played high school football. He not only played but absolutely loved the game. He participated in other sports, too—wrestling (for quicker reactions), track (for endurance and to become faster), and powerlifting (for strength gain)—but his focus was always to become better at football. His number was #54 for most of middle school, Junior Varsity, and Varsity years. While going through his personal belongings, I found that number everywhere: in his passwords, notes to himself, padlock combinations, just to name a few. And now it is the number that Justin uses to let us know that he is near.

Still trying to wrap my mind around this loss, I read books on grief. I joined some online chat groups. I talked to friends. I attended any and all ceremonies honoring the military and honoring Justin, trying desperately to find a place to connect, someone or something to tell me the secret to surviving the loss of a child.

It helped that others were hearing from Justin, too. A "brother," Justin's friend and roommate, called to tell me of one of his experiences that happened shortly after Justin left. Wil was sitting in his living room with his cell phone on the counter in the kitchen. He heard a text notification but did not get up to see who it was from, or what it was. It turns out that it was a text from Justin's sister, Morgan. Wil continued to ignore the text. Within seconds, his phone fell from the counter and slid the 15 feet or so to the living room. Many others have shared their experiences: dreams, #54 sightings, "coincidences," and so on. Hearing these experiences also helped validate my own.

It was early December 2012, and the Christmas holiday would soon be upon us. This would be the first Christmas without Justin, and I was dreading it, feeling heavy with emotion. Every year from the time Justin enlisted, with one exception (a deployment kept him from being home until early January), Justin was home for Christmas. For the past seven years, a two-week period revolved entirely around Justin, filled with friends, parties, and family, always leaving my schedule open in the event he had a spare moment for me. And I was not alone. Justin would make time for all of us. He took his sisters and niece tubing at a local ski hill and to the movies. Many of his high school friends would also plan to be home at Christmas, and they also were able to spend time with him. This year would be different, so different, and I was struggling with the emptiness I was feeling.

One morning, I woke before my alarm with an urgent need to check my email. This was not the first time I felt this urgency, and when I followed my intuition, I would find that something or someone needed my immediate attention. This day was no different.

My eyes landed on an email from my long-time friend, Linda. Linda and her family had relocated to Colorado earlier in the year, about a month before we lost Justin. The email from her was of her recent visit with a local medium, Sarina Baptista. She explained to me how she had wanted to find someone like this since her dad passed away several years before. More recently, she lost her niece in a car accident. And now Justin. Linda had heard about a medium in her area and, as a birthday gift to herself, scheduled a session requesting to connect to all three: her dad, Hailey, and Justin. In her email, Linda stated that she was able to connect with her niece, and it seemed that her dad was waiting in the background for the kids to go first. When Justin was asked to step forward, Sarina stated that there was SO much energy that she asked the other spirits to step back! Justin had plenty to say to Linda and asked that she share it with me. He wanted me to know that he was okay and that the place where he is now is more beautiful than one could possibly imagine, that he is always here for us, and that he was sorry that so many of his final estate matters had landed in my lap. Once he was sure Linda had all of his messages, he stepped back, and her dad came forward.

I was so moved by Linda's email. My boy was OKAY! HE IS OKAY! I shed tears of relief, instantly knowing that all those conversations I had with him in my head were very real, and I was immediately at peace. MY BOY IS OKAY!

I set the email aside and began my day, but I really could not get it off my mind. There was so much information that Justin had shared, and I was eager to go over it again and again. The underlying fear I had felt earlier completely dissipated, and I was thrilled to learn that I would never, ever have to say goodbye to my son.

I printed the email and shared it with Justin's dad and sisters. That message was the beginning. It provided hope and comfort, and the promise of more to come.

I was eager to learn more about the spiritual connection. I ordered Sarina's book for myself and one for each of my daughters. I printed Linda's email and tucked it in each book, eager to share my newly found source. I reviewed Sarina's website and learned that she was offering an online group for parents who had lost children, and I signed up for it. This was quite typical of how I approach things—in the background, observing and learning before deciding my next move.

I finally decided to book my own session, and that session was held coincidentally on the first anniversary of Justin's transition. I know now that there is no such thing as a coincidence. My first session was as emotionally moving and healing as when I read Linda's email. Justin was okay, and I was able to communicate quite easily with him through Sarina. Sarina commented on how far he had "advanced," as souls do, in such a short period of time. I learned that there is a growth period when one crosses over. I also learned that there is no concept of time there, so the soul progresses as it is ready. I also learned that we are all energy, both on this side of the wall and the other, which is how we can continue to communicate. If I worked to bring my own energy up to a higher level, I would be able to communicate with Justin more clearly. And that is what I set out to do.

The first action I took was writing in a gratitude journal to help raise my vibration. I cannot state strongly enough how much I did not want to do this. What could I possibly be grateful for, and, if I could clear my head to look around at all I had, should I feel grateful? I mean, is it right for me to be grateful in the wake of such an enormous loss? It almost felt wrong to me. Nevertheless, if this would help me to communicate with my boy, then that is what I was going to do. I also began to meditate, and I read everything I could get my hands on about grieving mothers, soul energy, and the journey of the soul. I was excited about the possibility, but I still was not sure I would be able to communicate as clearly and as confidently as Sarina.

Not everyone around me shared my excitement, however. I was careful with whom I shared this information and even those most trusted individuals would look at me as if to say, "Oh, poor Vickie. Her grief is so extreme that now she's hearing things." A handful close to me were inquisitive, somewhat curious, and kind. At the time I felt what I was learning was in question, and sometimes, disbelief. Looking back, I can see that the reactions I received were clearly a reflection of where that individual was at that particular time with their spiritual journey. Mostly, though, I kept my newly learned information to myself. I had complete faith in what I was learning and had little time and zero energy to spend on those that questioned the validity.

Even with this new hope, the earthly me continued to grieve. My family was grieving. The entire community was grieving, and all of this was draining me personally. This, of course, was counterproductive to my ability to connect. It was so conflicting—this heavy grief with the glimmer of hope, of possibility.

Still, this was the first time in months that a little light was able to break through the darkness. I continued training with Sarina and others, always focusing on improving my connection. A few years later, I joined Sarina in Lily Dale, New York, where she was holding a workshop. We attended an open gathering in a wooded park-like location where mediums offered their messages from the other side to various people in attendance. Of course, Justin made an appearance! Afterward, Sarina and I were walking back to our car, discussing the experience, and I heard Justin say, "You can totally do this, Mom." I can? It had not occurred to me to connect with others; my goal was to be able to talk with my son.

I had also scheduled a session for a medium onsite at Lily Dale. I had not had an in-person session before, and I was also curious to experience how Justin would come through with someone else. One of the early comments from this medium was, "I can see that you are a gifted healer." I was shocked and overwhelmed with questions. My focus in learning had been to improve my connection with Justin, and it had not occurred to me that I would be able to connect with others, or offer help with their healing. Learning this moved me to another focus, and to another level of my journey.

Carrie

Once I finally worked through the haze of my grief, I began having productive meditations. At this point in my experience, I was still using my original method of visualizing a door that opens onto a field with a path. This was the method my mother and I learned from a local group of women with whom we had worked before she got sick. One of the women would talk us through the meditation after a prayer for protection by having us relax and bring the white light through our heads and into our bodies. Then, she would tell us to visualize a door that opened to a field with a path to a swing. She told us to walk to the swing and invite whomever we wished to see to join us. I struggled with the visualization for years because I focused too much on the details. What does the door look like? Is there a fence around the field? What was the path like? Was it a dirt path or a stone path? I spent most of my time struggling to create this vision and answering those questions instead of focusing on my intentions and purpose for meditating in the first place. I couldn't quiet my mind enough. Also, I wasn't terribly consistent about practicing or attending the groups. I would get so frustrated when other people shared what they had seen and experienced during meditation, and I was still deciding on whether there were flowers in the field. It should go without saying, I did not have many productive meditation experiences, and I never had any visitors.

However, I kept practicing on my own here and there once my mom passed, and I started "getting" my mom. I could see her at the pond, gardening, which was one of her favorite things to do. She would have on a big floppy hat and her white blouse with little straw blue flowers on it. She would turn and wave to me, and I'd promptly dissolve into tears. Then, my mother's image would disappear along with the field, and so would my focus. It was a start, though, and I was determined to keep going.

As I kept practicing, I was particularly struck by the details that filled in on their own. That was very new. The path and field grew with new details that I did not think about or create. They just were. These encounters didn't come from me; they came *to* me. This gave me the encouragement to keep trying. And, as I did, it became second nature. I didn't have to think about the door, it was just there. I opened it onto the field, and there would be new flowers growing, or the grass would be higher and darker green, as if the seasons were passing. Everything became sharper, more distinct, and automatic.

Then, a month before the third anniversary of my mother's passing, I was watching an episode of *Psychic Investigators*, thinking how incredible it would be to marry two of my interests—the world of Spirit and mysteries. I was marveling at how people could help with a missing person's case or help families who needed answers about a loved one. After an episode or two, I decided to go to sleep, and as I was getting comfortable, my friend and coworker's six-year-old son, Amos, "popped" into my mind, much like my grandmother had the day of my mom's cancer diagnosis. Only this time, I could hear him. I could also see him more clearly and fully. I had never met this child. He had passed long before I met his mother. He gave me a detailed message to give to his mom who was going through a very difficult time. Once he finished, a coworker's mother who had recently passed gave me a message for her daughter. Well, that's not entirely true; Amos was practically pushed out of the way by my coworker's mother. She was a forceful personality who insisted I write down her message, which helped me to realize I wasn't just dreaming! I got up and got a notebook and a pen, and wrote down everything she wanted me to pass on to her daughter.

After she moved on, my grandmother came through with a message for my aunt. Then, I had a visit from my new boss's father. Each visit was very distinct, and each spirit had a very definite energy and personality. Each spirit had a different voice, or different way of communicating with me. I could see them, hear them, or just know what they wanted me to pass on. Eventually, the visitors quieted down, and I was able to sit with my amazement at what had just occurred. Then, the next morning, I had a very soft and musical visit from my neighbor's mother while I was getting ready for work.

For the most part, I knew that everyone who had received a message would be open to hearing about my experience and receiving that message. The next day, I relayed the messages I had received for my two co-workers. I was determined to not tell my new boss about my visit from his father because I was certain he would send me home out of fear for my mental health. However, my friend assured me she had talked to him about spiritual experiences before, and that he was very open to it. I didn't have any choice but to tell him, though, because when I took my break, his father yelled at me and told me to go tell his son the message he gave him. The message was well-received. Some much-needed validation was given when I described how I "saw" his father and my boss pulled a picture out of his desk. He was just as I described him, only older looking in the picture!

Many of the messages had parts that did not make sense to me but clearly made sense to the person for whom they were meant. For example, my grandmother made motions like she was conducting a symphony, which seemed strange to me. But when I described it to my aunt, she exclaimed that she was thinking of taking singing lessons, but she had been hesitant to do so. Clearly, my grandmother was telling her to take the lessons! I was amazed at how Spirit was able to personalize the messages so that the person receiving the message had validation, but I did, too. Trusting the message was the hardest part for me; I kept wondering if it was just my imagination. I truly felt like an instrument relaying information, and it was largely information I knew nothing about. I just needed to describe everything I heard, saw, or understood to each recipient. The message was for them. I was just the messenger.

Of course, I was absolutely exhilarated by this development. I had no idea how it happened, or why it happened. I hadn't even tried! They just came to me. One day, shortly after, I was sharing the experience with my sister-in-law, and my seven-year-old nephew was listening in. He had been visiting with my deceased grandfather and had given us a message or two from my mother. He stopped playing and said, "It happened because you asked for it." I thought back to that night and knew he was correct. I had been thinking about how incredibly amazing it would be to have that skill, so I was given a taste!

I began meditating a bit more. It got easier to visualize my field and pond, and I was seeing my mother more. I still couldn't communicate much with her because I was still missing her so badly. I was getting impressions of general information, but it wasn't making sense to me. I still would get overwhelmed by grief, but it wasn't as invasive. I even had an interesting meditation experience where I was standing in front of the door that opened onto my pasture, and a great figure was waiting for me. I can only explain that I recognized this to be an angel of some sort, very large and comforting in a protective way. The angel reached out for my hand and escorted me to my pasture. Then, when I turned the angel was gone. Nothing was said. I just felt protected. However, in February, just as I was finding my footing in many aspects of my life—grief over my mother's passing, life as a new "empty nester" with a son in his third year in college, and a daughter in her first, starting to think about what I wanted my next stage of life to look like, my 21-year-old son, Chase, died. My world was completely shattered.

Kim

As I think back now over the years, I remember several things that I "witnessed" after a death that were forgotten, rationalized away, or dismissed. I know now that these were loved ones reaching out to show or tell me that they were okay. Over 30 years ago my uncle came to me the night after he passed as a beam of light that landed on my leg spreading warmth throughout my whole body. A breeze blew through the dog pen a day after one of my dogs passed while the air remained still outside the wire pen. I saw a beam of light through which my mom's soul departed the hospital room soon after her body stopped breathing. But it took Dan's passing for me to acknowledge and believe in our ability to connect to those on the other side.

Dan has told me that he is always here with me and our dogs. I don't always feel his presence, but one of our dogs does. Soon after Dan passed, our dog Bella, with whom Dan was very close, started making a funny sound. I would catch her occasionally staring toward the doorway of the room we were in while making this sound. It was a sound I had never heard from her before. I learned that Bella was seeing what I could not and recognized Dan, but wasn't used to his new form, thus the strange sound. So, I would say "It's just daddy. He is here checking on us," and she would stop making the noise. I asked Dan for help during the recuperation after Bella's surgery, and he said that he would talk to her about what she needed to do. As a result, this very rambunctious dog remained perfectly still and followed my direction until her knees were healed.

Dan continued to send the message that he was there with me, but he knew that I would need a sign from him to really believe it. He said that he would show me by drawing something on the mirror in our bathroom. I couldn't believe he was saying that because he knew I took very short showers and it was a big bathroom. There wouldn't be time for any steam or drawings to appear on the mirror. But sure enough, from then on, every time I stepped out from one of my 5-minute showers, a huge set of angel wings spanned the top of the five-foot mirror in our bathroom. At first, I couldn't believe what I was seeing but as time went on, I started trusting his messages more and more.

At first, his messages felt very random and a bit clumsy. As I thought about it, I finally realized that he was learning, too, and looking for ways to effectively communicate with me just as I was learning to receive and interpret what he was trying to communicate. He was testing if I could see, hear, smell, and feel the messages he was sending. Soon after the changes to our mirror, he started to sketch the same wings on the sides of the two planters that were on the railing of our front porch. One day I said, "You are ruining the planters!" and the drawing stopped. Another time, I was standing folding laundry in the exact spot on our bed where he used to do the same task. There was a basket of supplements on the corner of the dresser behind me. It started to sound as if someone were slowly shaking one of the bottles from side to side. I said, "I hear you," and it stopped.

Although I was still very deep in grief, it was becoming increasingly difficult to ignore the signs he was sending me. I heard a few noises early on, some of which initially scared me but later became part of my life. There were two instances where he kept plants alive far longer than they should have lived. Once, I was leaving for a vacation and couldn't water the plants from his funeral for two weeks. These were plants that needed to be watered every other day. I quietly said "If the plants are alive when I get back then they will be and if not, so be it." When I returned, the soil was rock hard but the plants were green and beautiful. I even had a single rose that was given to me at a yoga class live for nearly 3 months. Dan knew how much I loved flowers!

Another undeniable moment was when he sent me a message through another person. I was visiting my father's and his grave with another family member. Dan's grave was our last stop, and we had just gotten back into the car. I asked her where she wanted to eat, and she used a nickname that Dan had for a restaurant that no one else knew but me. I asked her why she said that, and she said she didn't know. I asked her to describe the restaurant she was talking about, and she did. There was no doubt that Dan had spoken a private message to me through her.

Others saw Dan with me after he passed. One of the ways I processed the grief was to get help from an energy worker, who it turned out, lived in my neighborhood. I actually reached out to her for something totally different, and she ended up helping me with my grief. She said she saw Dan in the corner of the room and described his energy to a tee. She said his energy was wrapped around me, holding me, like nothing she had seen before. And I felt him with me. One time, during a meditation, he was trying to encourage me to let go of him as I knew him, and I could feel him holding my hand. During a full moon meditation where I traveled to the moon, he went with me and we danced on the moon together, just as we had done so many times before in our living room.

I'm not really sure of the exact date that I began to view the world differently, but it started soon after Dan passed. My desire to stay connected to him opened up a whole new world that I am still learning about. I don't know why this particular loss brought my life to such a devastating and screeching halt, but I do know that the crazy, busy life I was living was never going to lead me to my purpose. The complete disintegration of my life as I had known it forced me to find a different way, a better way, to live. It forced me to accept and love a brokenness that in the past, I would have shunned. All of the emptiness and silence allowed me to find and love my authentic self and to recreate my life. Dan said it almost immediately after he died, that he wanted me to find and live my purpose. He wasn't going to tell me what that was, but he was going to support me in my journey to find it. And so he did.

Sarina

"You are the bridge between this world and the next." Those were the words from the very first medium with whom I ever spoke after J.T. left. For months, I had been searching for the "why." Why did he leave? Why did he have to go? Why did my family have to endure this nightmare?

Prior to this call with the medium in September 2007, I had been on a quest to find these answers. I would stare out J.T.'s bedroom window at night and ask, "Where are you? I know you are out there somewhere. Where? How can I find you again?"

Only a few days after his passing, I received my first message from him. It was through a friend's mother. I had been sitting at my desk, running those same questions over and over in my head. I knew the answers were out there, but where? Then a list of names and phone numbers caught my eye. This was a list of all of our friends and family. I printed it just a few days prior so whoever was going to make those dreaded calls that J.T. was gone had a current contact list. I stared at the paper. "Someone knows. Someone knows why."

Throughout my life, I had been getting those "hits" as they call them. This one was so strong. It was almost like a force outside of myself was guiding me, pushing me to look. *Look at the list,* is what I heard in my head. I ran my finger down the list and stopped on a name. It was my friend's mother, who I might have met twice in my life. She met J.T. maybe once. This certainly wasn't someone with whom I had ever had conversations about esoteric subjects. I called the number, and her husband answered. I said, "This is Sarina." He said, "Hold on." Within moments, she was on the phone. I said one word. "Why?" She said, "Funny you should call because J.T. visited me last night, and he has a message for you. Go get a pen and paper." Stunned, I grabbed the first paper I could find. She continued, "I did not want you to see me leave. You were the perfect mom. You did everything perfectly. I had to go. I tried twice before to leave, but I could not leave you. This time I had to go."

In just those few sentences, J.T. answered the questions burning in my brain. Of course, I had many more, but knowing he was okay and able to communicate with others kept me going those very hard days. I became an intuitive sponge. I would ask anyone and everyone I knew who had even the slightest intuitive abilities if they had received any messages from him. I also was so confused and frustrated that he didn't come to me. Why was I not able to communicate with him? Why was he going to everyone else? Or so it felt. Another dear friend, Monika, heard from him also. He told her to tell me he has big plans for me. I believe I picked something up and threw it across the room at this point, so frustrated. "WHAT?" I yelled back. "WHAT PLANS?"

It was August 2007, just five months after J.T. left, when I knew that I was hot on the trail of "my plan." Through some amazing synchronicities, I found myself reading "Power of the Soul" written by a wonderful medium, John Holland. I had never been to a medium, and although I believed wholeheartedly in their abilities, I just didn't know enough about them to understand it completely.

As I read the description of the clairs, which is how we receive information from Spirit, it hit me. I could do this. I could be a medium. Could this be it? Could this be the "big plans"?

The following day, I was having lunch with a dear friend, and I told her about my discovery. Still in disbelief that I might be able to help others in this truly incredible way, and that I might be able to reconnect with my son, I said, "Well, we'll see. I'm going to need a pretty big sign to convince me." Right after our lunch, I went to the store down the street to pick up some toiletries. I had recently broken my toe, and it was incredibly painful to walk. I decided to use one of the motorized carts to get around. I was in the toothpaste aisle when an older lady approached me and asked, "Excuse me, where are the curlers?"

I clearly was not a store employee, however, she asked as if I was, like I, in a motorized cart, was working in the toothpaste aisle incognito. Happily, I told her the curlers were one aisle over, waited for her to go, and then laughed hysterically. There was my sign. In John Holland's book, he listed the ways you can tell you are psychic, and one of them was that people in stores approach you as if you are an employee and ask where items are in the store. Thinking back, this has happened to me quite often, but this particular time, it changed my life. As I sat there laughing at the Universe's humorous response to my sign request, I was immediately humbled. Could I really be psychic?

One week later, I had my session with a medium. She was recommended to me by a dear friend. It was a phone session, as she was in California, and I was in Colorado. I hadn't told her about J.T., and I had no idea what to expect. She began the call with "my guides" giving her information about me. She said they were showing her a contract with very thick ink, and she asked if we were signing any contracts. I said no. She said, "Oh, this is *your* contract. Did you know you are a medium, like me? You are the bridge between this world and then next." Stunned at the verification of what I discovered at the store the prior week, I asked "How?

27

How does this happen? How do I get there?" She replied, "Training, training, training. Your guides say you can hear them." I said, "No, I can't hear them." In my mind I'm thinking she's nuts and just making stuff up now. At that moment, in my head, I heard in a very strong male voice, "Yes, you can hear us." I guess I can hear them, but oh my God, what does that even mean?

    She suggested I start training right away. There was a psychic center about an hour away from me at the time, so I took their introductory class and began my journey. It felt so hard in the beginning, like I was never going to get there. About a month after my medium session, I found a local mentor who offered one-on-one training. Everything happened very quickly after that. Within a month, I was receiving messages from kids on the other side. It wasn't clear, by any means, but I struggled through it, doing my homework, practicing connecting every day. I loved being able to help other parents, but still longed to hear my son again.

Chapter Three
Together Again

Vickie

Justin is part of my day, every day. I heard and felt him immediately, but it took some time for me to trust that it was truly him. I expected to feel a void when he left, one that would match the hole in my heart. Instead of a void, I felt as if he were near. I struggled to understand how that could be possible, wondering if what I felt was part of my grief. I was so relieved when I learned that what I felt was Justin's presence. Just as when he was here with us, he worked hard, was consistent and persistent in getting through to me. As time went on, I realized he was here, a part of me, a part of my day, and ever so present. Some days I connect with him purposefully in mediation, but most days he pops in and out of my awareness.

He also often visits me in my dreams. In one, I was outside a building that had a large staircase leading to the entrance. I had climbed to the top and stopped, looking out, as if I were waiting for someone. There were several other people at the bottom and climbing the stairs, walking past me and entering the building. I noticed a man in a red hooded sweatshirt quickly approaching and then climbing the stairs. As he came closer, I could see his face. It was Justin! He scooped me up into one of his famous bear hugs, and I felt tears streaming down my face. Man, I miss those hugs!

Justin has such a strong presence that we often refer to him as "Mr. Bossy Pants." By "we," I mean myself as well as anyone who knew him. At one of my granddaughter's high school basketball games, I purchased a string of raffle tickets for the 50-50 prize. The last ticket ended with the number 54. I looked at my nephew sitting next to me and said, "I'm going to win." And I did. Another time Justin popped into his sister Adrienne's awareness, and she said "What!?" out loud, a little impatient. Her daughter, about three at the time, asked "What did you say, Mom?" Adrienne said something like, "Oh, nothing. Uncle Bubba is messing with me." This little girl, who had not met Justin, said, "That Uncle Bubba is SO bossy, right Mom?"

Brett, a teammate of Justin's, brought his family for a visit, and he suggested we go sky diving, or "go jump," as he and Justin called it. This was something they did often as part of their "job," and I was excited for the opportunity to experience it. Brett, my sister, Val, and I agreed to go. Val had jumped a couple of times before, but this would be my first time. Despite my inexperience and the fact that I would be voluntarily leaving an airplane, I didn't feel nervous or afraid. In contrast, I felt very calm. It was a beautiful day and a beautiful area along the Lake Michigan shoreline where we met our guide. We were relaxed and joking with the guides as the plane gained altitude. Brett jumped first, solo, and then my sister jumped tandem with her guide, and finally me tandem with my guide. It began with a fast, free-falling drop and then the parachute opened, and we simply floated down to the ground. I could see Brett and Val below me, and I felt peaceful, enjoying the beauty of the lakes and landscape. It was incredibly beautiful.

We landed, I was handed the picture package I had purchased, and we left the terminal. We had a relaxed drive home, stopping for dinner along the way. It was a few days before I had an opportunity to view the photos and, as I was looking at them, one caught my eye. It was taken from inside the airplane, overlooking the wing and showed a very clear shadow—a silhouette—of Justin sitting on the wing of the airplane. I could not believe my eyes! I emailed the photo to Linda (my trusted anchor) to see if it was just me or if I really saw him. She responded immediately, and said she saw him too! It was no wonder that I was completely calm; Justin had been with us the entire time.

As a family, we struggle each year with how to handle the anniversary of the day of Justin's departure. We began with a large, public celebration to honor him, followed by an informal gathering to celebrate him. As the years pass, it continues to be a difficult day, and we have all agreed that we also needed some privacy to just "be" with the day. Recently a high school friend of Justin's brought an idea to us: a Memorial 5K Fun Run. The race would be in the morning and would finish midday, leaving us with the time we all needed.

Justin was an athlete known for his hard work and tenacity, so the idea of a competitive athletic event to celebrate him was perfect! The early hours of the day of the event brought a thunderstorm. "Really, Justin?" I thought. "After all of this planning, are we going to have to call it over the weather?" After all, he both entered this world and said his farewell with a roll of thunder, so I should not have been surprised. An hour or so before the race, the clouds parted, and the sun came out. It was a beautiful, cool morning (perfect race weather, I was told) and there were 154 pre-registered runners. Many of his high school friends attended, and I could overhear their stories of how they trained for the race. Every one of them told a story of how Justin was encouraging him, in his own unique (and, at times, ruthless) way, to train harder. It was so heartwarming, and truly a beautiful event.

Justin and I also work together in helping others to connect. Sometimes this is done without my planning. Once I attended a class of what I thought was my pre-registered training with Sarina. The class had been on my mind all day, and I was really looking forward to it. I logged on at the designated time, and Sarina was surprised to see me. The class I logged on to was not the class I had intended, but another class. Sarina encouraged me to stay as Justin was already present, and we assisted Sarina and JT with the training.

We were asked to write our bios to include with this book. Before beginning, I asked Justin for his help. I began writing, but I wasn't happy with how it was going. Finally, frustrated, I asked Justin, "Okay, *you* tell me what to write." I closed my eyes and began typing the words he gave me:

"Vickie Hays is audacious and my momma. She loves me with her whole heart, and I love her. She is fulfilling her purpose by communicating her experiences to others. She is awesome. And loud. And perfect. With a million-dollar smile and a laugh that I love. She is my momma."

This made me laugh! And cry. What an incredible young man I have been blessed with to travel this journey. As hard as it is for this human momma to be here without her son, I am so grateful to have him by my side.

Carrie

When my son died, the pain blocked everything. All the progress I had made with meditation and actively connecting with Spirit just stopped. I felt Spirit around me at the time, but I didn't initiate any of the connections. Somehow, I was guided and protected through the first days of my grief. For instance, during the visitation at the funeral home, I could feel the love and prayer of the community like a palpable force that surrounded me. It kept me standing and moving through the day. I knew there was a greater force guiding the decisions I had to make, and this force moved me through the social obligations that come with funerals. I felt that the choices I made for the service—what my son wore, and even what I said at some points—were coming from a higher place. However, this guidance that cushioned me was not something I asked for; it was just there. Even though I wanted to reach my son, and I felt that loving guidance around me, I still couldn't fight the grief to connect. For months, I didn't have it in me to do any meditation with intention at all.

It wasn't until July of that year that I felt able to reach out in some way. As my mother and I had always gone to Lily Dale, NY to visit and listen to mediums, I decided that I should go there to attempt to reach Chase. In looking up information, I had come upon a session with Sarina that highlighted her communication with her son on the other side. This intrigued me, so I signed up with a friend who had lost a son as well. We had even bought Sarina's book and read it in preparation for our class with her.

Sarina's session had us completely enthralled. Some of it was familiar, as my mother used to talk about the contract our soul signs before we come to earth in this form. However, I was having a hard time buying that I had chosen to be a chubby, broke, elementary teacher who lost a son. I figured I had been late for the "picking" and told them to just give me what was left over! I was frustrated and very upset at the thought that Chase and I had chosen to take on these roles. Yet, I learned a great deal and had intentions of working through Sarina's exercises to connect. However, once at home again, life and grief swallowed me up, and I didn't make it very far. I was still really struggling to survive this enormous loss. Meditation was not possible at the time, because I felt so broken. Eventually, my mind would wander back to the work of J.T. and Sarina, and I'd want to try again. This cycle of trying and failing continued, and meditation stayed on the back burner until about two years later when Sarina was back at Lily Dale. When I saw her listed in the program, I booked private readings for my daughter and me.

During my reading, Sarina insisted that she knew I had connected to Spirit before and that I still could. I was quick to tell her that I was completely blocked by grief. It was so upsetting to me that I'd "lost" that ability when I lost my son, but Sarina assured me that I hadn't! She guided me through meditation to construct an octahedron, which was very new and completely foreign to me, but the moment I did, my son was with me! As soon as I invited him in, he filled the shape in such a real way that I could physically feel him hugging me. The khaki pants on his six-foot-seven frame were so vivid that I could see the weave of the threads in the fabric. I could see each glossy strand of his hair and the softness of the expression in his eyes. The whole space filled with his presence. I'm not a terribly imaginative person, so I knew this was him. I couldn't have concocted such intense detail on my own. This was my son! I could physically feel him and see him! Then, he told me that he loved me, and I was so relieved and moved and excited, all at once.

    I am still working to reach Chase more fluently, and working with Sarina, Kim, and Vickie has strengthened my connection with him. As we meditate together, and when I meditate on my own, I can communicate with him more and more. Early on, when I was reading about Sarina and her experience, I would chide Chase and say, "Hey, look at J.T.! *He* is helping his mother…where are you, buddy?" He's been sure to let me know that I was the one holding up the process!

    I won't lie and tell you that I'm happy he is there, or that this beautiful communication is worth his physical loss. I'm a human mother, here on earth, and I miss having my boy here. I adore him, and I wish that I was watching him get his first job, get married, and become a father. For some reason, I have been devastated at the thought that I would never dance with him at his wedding. However, he knows that, and one of the first times I was able to really reach him, he danced with me. It was during one of our writing group meditations, and I had been rushing around that day. I was trying to pull a "Zoom meeting" outfit together, wondering how important it was that I looked nice. So, when I meditated and got to him, he immediately indicated that I wasn't dressed for the occasion. He had always been a sharp dresser! During this connection, he was dressed in a tuxedo, and he twirled me around to the most lively, beautiful music. It was such a lovely confirmation that our connection is real and that he knows what I need.

    One of the most important things I've learned from him is that I should have no guilt about his death. As bereaved parents, there is so much guilt that comes with that role…even if there is no possible way you could be responsible. Chase has assured me of that. And, he has assured me that he is fine. It has taken a few visits for me to see that and understand. So, now, with him, I am learning about our journey and how the universe works. He has helped me to understand the importance of love and our time here. I'm very grateful to be able to reach him and see some of his work on the plane that he is now. Recently, I was able to witness him helping my very ill niece, Elizabeth, cross over. He showed me that they were walking through a field of flowers, and she was well there, able to walk and sing, and her physical features were unmarred by her genetic condition. They were bathed in such love and joy that it seems silly that we could feel sad they are there. Chase also showed this scene to my other brother who has struggled with the loss of a niece and a nephew. My brother said he had been dreaming that Chase was holding Elizabeth's hand in a field and that she looked so much better. I described the scene to him and told him he was receiving confirmation that there is life after we leave here.

While I'm not "over" my son's passing, I'm still standing. I'm still communicating with him and learning from him. We are still loving each other and taking care of each other…he's just the one who has more experience now. He will "pop in" when I'm driving and hold my hand when I hear a song that he used to play on his guitar. I can feel it like he is in the car with me. He lets me miss him, when the grief comes in, but he doesn't let it go on for too long. He keeps reminding me that there is much more to do, and too much to enjoy, to spend any time missing him…especially when he has been right here all along!

Kim

In the beginning, once I knew he was there, I was reluctant to make decisions without his input and relied heavily on what he thought was best for me. After all, he had a much better view and surely knew more about how I should proceed than I did. This was a strange feeling for me to be that dependent on someone else. I had always been a very independent person. Dan was learning his new role, too, and I just wasn't ready for some of his suggestions. After all, I was still grieving, and not ready to move on to something new quite so quickly. I did interview for a new job, which he said would be boring. I now know what he was saying. He was saying that it was the old way of doing things, not the new way, and that it wasn't a good fit for my newfound purpose. So, I sold our house, forgot

Finding Love and Purpose

about finding a job right then, and moved about a mile away. Dan said that I should make my new home "mine" and not put out pictures and memorials for him like I had in our old house. It took him a while to initiate a visit at the new place I was renting, which initially concerned me. I now know he was just pushing us "out of the nest" of dependency, and wanted the pups and I to build our own new life there. Minimizing his participation in the process helped promote excitement and adventure and limited the sadness and feeling of loss. I know he was cheering us on with every new decision we encountered.

He does initiate a visit to the new place when he wants to encourage me to stay on track for what is ahead. Because he limits the times when he pops in, it makes it so much more impactful when he does. It's like he is using an exclamation point to get my attention and stress the importance of my focus or decision. I know he is always nearby if I need him and very anxious to support us on our new path.

Dan continued to help me with things such as making sure his old car passed the emissions test so I could register it in my name and eventually sell it. He gave the thumbs up on a new car I found, so I would have more reliable transportation. He was also in favor of accepting the offer on our house but less impressed with where I hastily decided to move. I probably should have asked a few more questions about that. We had lots of conversations as I was wading through the mounds of paperwork he had saved, thanking him for being so organized and scolding him for hoarding every paper that had ever come across his desk and using so many paper clips. I painfully let go of most of his stuff during that move, but in the end, his "things" didn't matter.

While a lot of the information I have received from Dan has been to help me to discover and make time for my newfound purpose, which I will talk about later, some of his communications have been very practical, and felt so familiar, that they made me smile. Procrastination and being too busy have always been a problem for me. One night, while writing was still on the "to-do" list for a chapter of this book and the deadline was looming, Dan showed up twice. He usually visits monthly, if that, and here he visited twice in one day to make sure I was writing. Thank you, sweetheart!

One place I felt Dan come in regularly was during monthly meditations with Sarina. Although each one of her sessions is unique, in preparing for each adventure, she has us build an octahedron in which to "travel." We build the octahedron with roses. She has us put a rose at each of the six points and then connect them. But mine always had 12 roses. Dan's first gift to me was one pink and one red rose, so instead of a single rose at the points of my octahedron, I would always see two roses—one red and one pink. As time went on, the color of the pink rose would become bolder and the red rose began to fade. Every so often, he would encourage me to try a new color rose to signify the change happening within me. If I really needed him there, the red rose would always show up, but it was becoming less and less vibrant. At first, this felt scary to me, but over time I realized that he wasn't leaving me. He was encouraging me to practice and strengthen my gifts on my own. The last time I saw the red rose, while writing this book, it had become shriveled and dried. I think he is telling me that I don't need him like I once did and am now able to stand on my own.

Although I know Dan is always with me, he has become less and less willing to lead me to decisions. Early on, I think he wanted to help me so much that he was trying to expeditiously do things for me like help me find a job or a place to live. That only led to frustration for us both. He would say things like "write" and "meditate," but in the emotional state I was in, he might as well have said, "Go find a blue cow." I wasn't thinking clearly and couldn't seem to make the simplest of decisions, so it felt good that he was at least throwing some ideas and actions out for me to ponder. As time has passed, though, he has only occasionally mentioned options or said nothing at all when I asked him what he thought I should do about something. At first, I couldn't understand why he was doing this. But now I believe that this was his attempt at helping me believe in myself and become less dependent on him. I can almost hear him say "Go meditate and see how it feels to *you*." I think we needed a clean break from the physical and emotional relationship we once had in order to begin again in our new, more spiritual relationship. Although initially frustrating, his silence at times forced me to look in other places for guidance and to make decisions for myself. He knew I was capable of taking care of myself; he was just letting me come to the same conclusion. Whereas, in the beginning, I would only ask him a question or two for help, now I feel comfortable tossing out those questions to others who may be in a better position to help me in that particular situation. I have realized that he is not the only one looking out for me. For instance, I now have an animal guide, a dolphin named Matilda, who has taught me how to bring joy back into my life and always makes me smile when I see her. So, I guess you could say that our relationship has matured. As close as we were when he was physically here, it is becoming so much more now. He was, and is, my soul mate. At every step, he has encouraged me to move on and find my joy rather than get stuck in what once was. More importantly, as time goes on, I'm getting better at accepting his gift of freedom to find my own way into the future.

Sarina

It seems like yesterday when I first heard my son's voice in my head, yet it also feels like decades ago. I was so frustrated that I could hear others' loved ones, but not my son. Of course, that was the overachiever in me. I'd only been in training for a few months and thought I should have fluid conversations with my son by now. I still had to rely on others for messages from my boy. How frustrating. What kind of medium was I anyway?

Every day, and I mean every day, I would practice receiving from my guides, my helpers, others' loved ones, others' guides. I knew in my heart that it would just click one day, but I wondered so many times, "Am I just making this up? What if this never happens? What if I go through all of this training and it doesn't work?" My human fears worked diligently to get the better of me. I still wasn't convinced I could do this work. I had such high expectations for myself. Receiving messages from kids on the other side did come very naturally and quickly. They were great communicators and definitely did the heavy lifting to help me understand their messages. I still had doubts it would ever feel like a conversation. It seemed so hard and far away.

During each of my psychic exercises, I would ask J.T. to come talk. In the beginning, I could hear maybe one word at a time. I used this to my advantage and told him to give me the first word of the sentence he wanted to share. Once I felt confident in that one word, I asked for the second, then the third, and so on, until I had a sentence. Painstakingly, I wrote every word down. It seemed like this took forever just to get one short sentence. Nonetheless, I continued with this exercise each day.

Most of our "conversations" were at my prompting. I would meditate, get clear and then ask him to come in. I felt I had to work so hard at getting to the right frequency that I needed to follow this "prescription" to ensure success. And it was working. I felt I was getting clearer and clearer each day. I kept setting my intention, "Conversations with J.T. flow and are easy. I hear him clearly. I receive clearly." I would say this intention probably twenty times each day.

J.T. was still communicating with me in other ways as I was learning to hear him. He would give me hugs when I would cry (which was quite often in that first year), and I could feel his little arms around my hips. He would also pull my hair, or rather tickle my scalp when he wanted to get my attention. It was always in the same place on my head, so I knew it was him. There were other kids also using these physical methods to get my attention, such as tickling my side, so J.T. knew he had to be unique so I would know it was him.

I remember so clearly one early evening driving down one of our two-lane roads, off in la-la land, not really paying attention to where I was or how fast I was going. I felt the tickle on my scalp. It was so intense that it really did feel like he was pulling my hair. I asked him if it was him, and very loudly in my head, I heard, "SLOW DOWN!" Well, that jarred me out of my stupor. I looked down at the speedometer and I was going fifteen miles per hour over the limit! I took my foot off the gas and coasted down to the speed limit. I came to a rise in the road, and right over the other side was a sheriff. I thanked J.T. for the literal wake-up call, and he said, "No problem, Mom." Startled that I heard him again, without prompting, without meditating, without clearing, and without setting intention, I said, "Whoa. Is that you?" "Of course, it's me!" and we continued to have a conversation for the duration of my car trip.

Just like that, I could hear him so clearly, like he was right there in the car with me, and just like that, the switch had flipped, and my intentions became reality.

From that moment on, we would have regular conversations as I drove around town. I would ask him questions about what he was doing, where he was, what I should be doing—anything and everything! I truly had my boy back, and I was on top of the world!

It felt like he had just returned from a long trip and was telling me all about his adventures. I absolutely loved our conversations. I couldn't believe I could hear him! It was so clear. All of those doubts over the last couple of months evaporated into the ether. I knew that, with him by my side, I could do anything. And it wasn't long before he made it abundantly clear that there was so much more work for me to do. He became my teacher, my guide, my helper, my confidant. When I would get frustrated, he was there to say, "It's all right, Mom. You'll get it. Keep trying." Some of my assigned tasks were so daunting. I would say, "Are you sure, J.T.? That seems like a stretch to me." "Have faith, Mom. You are not alone. We will be helping you!"

That became his mantra each time I would balk at the next project he'd give me, thinking I wasn't ready, didn't know enough, wasn't clear enough, or whatever other excuse I had. With his persistence and guidance, I pushed through all of my doubts and was helping so many others with their grief.

It was just a couple of months after our reconnection that he told me it was time to start meditation groups. I felt so awkward leading the meditations, thinking to myself, "Who do you think you are? You can't do this." And, of course, J.T. was right there saying, "Let us help! We will give you the words." As soon as I released my ideas of what I thought I was supposed to say, the words flowed through me.

It wasn't long into my journey when J.T. told me it was time to start training others. "What?! Are you kidding? I've only been training for a year! How do you expect me to teach others when I don't even know the answers myself?" "Ah, you forget, Mom. We are here. We are the teachers. We will teach through you." The light bulb went off in my head. Oh, so I don't have to be perfect and know everything. I just have to be a clear receiver. "I can do that!"

Chapter Four
Healing and Growth

Vickie

When my son left this world, I was devastated. My worst fears had come true. I had felt a heaviness when I learned of his enlistment in the Marine Corps and spent the next eight years on pins and needles, fearing the worst. Looking back, I knew in the beginning that this would be how he left this world. I now understand that Justin had to leave, but it has been a long road for me to reach that understanding.

When I received the news that Justin had been killed in action, it was as if I were watching a scene from a play transpire on a stage—something from someone else's life. It seemed so unreal. Most importantly, I didn't feel that he was missing. In fact, it was quite the opposite—I felt that he was very near to me. I questioned this, teetering between the reality that he was gone and the very strong sense of his presence. I wondered if this was denial, or possibly my grief not allowing me to believe he was gone.

Jon, a friend of Justin's, told us of a dream he had where Justin came to him and said, "I'm not really gone—I'm right here!" Jon interpreted this to be that Justin had not actually died; that it had been a mistake, or that we weren't being told the truth. I believe Justin's message was what I know to be true today: he is merely on the other side of a paper-thin wall, and is, in fact, very present.

During this time, I watched a popular television program called *Ghost Whisperer*. I heard Justin in my head saying, "That's not how it is, Mom. It's not like that." So, I wondered, how is it?

The desire to understand led me to learn about ideas that I had never even contemplated before. I learned about my guides and how they were here to help me in every aspect of my life. I also learned that my soul has a contract and, as crazy as it seems, I had agreed to all of the events that had transpired and to the people who participated. This was a very strange, and very painful, concept. It was also comforting to know that not only had I agreed to these events, but that Justin had agreed to them, too. It was part of our plan for him to leave, and he had chosen the circumstances in which to do that. He created his own plan. And it was even more comforting to know that he continues to be near me, encouraging and guiding me in his ever so subtle way. Okay, that is a joke. There never was, and never will be, anything subtle about Justin.

I had to learn to allow and accept the messages to come through, to trust that the messages were genuine, and to trust that anything I was hearing would be for my highest good. This meant that I didn't need to fear the consequences (from my religious upbringing) of listening to them. I began to believe in myself and to believe what I was receiving, that we are not alone, and that our guides are eager to assist us along this path. I began to understand that we are here to experience this life in order to learn and grow, and to perhaps heal from past-life experiences. We are to continue to grow and develop our souls to be more like the Divine. I call that Divine Power God; others call the Divine Power by other names, but it is all the same: Creator, Allah, Spirit, Yahweh, The Great Spirit, God.

I learned that the conversations in my head were genuine. I learned I was clairaudient—that I receive messages primarily by hearing. Through practice and mentoring, I was able to distinguish between my own thoughts and the messages I was receiving. I was eager to learn more, but wondered why. What was the purpose of this, and where was it taking me? Knowing that Justin's departure was part of my purpose made it even more important for me to find it.

I have, at times, questioned my abilities and my purpose. It contradicts my social circle, my family circle, and the religious teachings of my childhood. I had to face—and question—my fear of not following those childhood lessons. Justin helped me to understand that the beliefs I had were limiting and only part of the story. To understand that we are all energy makes it more complete. Not everyone in my world would agree, and that's okay. It is up to each of us to find our path. A friend described it perfectly when he told me, "There are many paths up the mountain, but the view at the top is the same."

I am extremely grateful that Justin is here with me every moment of every day. Knowing that he is always within reach helps me to accept his absence on Earth. Justin is the reason I am where I am today, and he is my guide.

While I am forever grateful for this journey, and that Justin and I are traveling it together, the human side of me still mourns the loss of my son. Justin was just 26 when he left this world. I sometimes wonder where he would be today. Would he have had a military career? (Possibly, although a friend told me he expected Justin to be President – he was *that* guy). Would he have married? Would he have children, my grandchildren? I sometimes daydream of what that would be like and I mourn the loss of those life events he will never experience. And then I'll hear him say, "I'm right here! Just reach out, Momma, and I'll hold your hand."

Carrie

For most people, it's counterintuitive to think that a great, catastrophic loss could be what heals you the most, but it does seem to be true for me. When my mom died, I began receiving messages from Spirit. All my fears of dying and worries about what happens next dissolved. I've seen the glorious light and joy in the faces of the people who have gone on. I see how they still hold on to their love—they know they are still loved, and they still love us. I have been shown that nothing matters but love. Then when I felt I understood how love goes on, I was tested further when my son died. I had to marry this knowledge that love goes on with the worst pain and loss a mother can experience. I struggled with so much anger and bitterness. I questioned everything again. Did I still think that what comes after this earthly life was so great? I had my doubts when the Universe took my beautiful boy from me.

Yet, when I was ready to let him in, connecting with Chase slowly helped me to accept his passing. At first, he helped me to stop questioning everything. I had been asking all the questions everyone asks after the loss of a loved one: Is he okay? Does he know I love him? What could I have done to keep him alive? Was I responsible for his passing? I was his mother; it was my job to keep him healthy. Heart issues and a night out celebrating a roommate's 21st birthday led to him being unresponsive the next morning. There was some debate between coroners about what the cause of death was, but in the end, the result was still the same. He is no longer physically here. I still have moments where I begin to head down that path of questioning and grief, but he always gives me something to readjust my focus. He helps me to remember all the good times and points out that I don't have to "miss" him because he is not gone.

Chase started to guide me by sending me songs to let me know that he was there or what direction I should take in a situation. He was a musician who performed locally, and he wrote, produced, played all the parts, and recorded an album in his college apartment weeks before he died. Music was our love language, so it was far more than a coincidence when a song came on that directly addressed something I had been thinking or questioning. Chase used songs to communicate what I needed to do after he passed—when to head back to work, to tell me he loved me, and once he even confirmed that it was time to let a beloved pet go. These conversations helped me to let him in and hear more from him.

Currently, Chase has been my guide through an interesting transition in my life. My daughter has graduated medical school and will be moving away for her residency in the next few weeks. In the same week as her graduation, she got married. So, in the same span of a few weeks, she has closed on her first house, got her residency placement (three and a half hours away), graduated, and got married. Any big event or life change is difficult as a bereaved parent because you really feel the loss and believe that your child's absence is more present than ever. In the meantime, one of Chase's best friends, Kevin, got married, which is incredibly hard to face because you wish your child was here to have those same life events. Then, my childhood home where my son, daughter, and I lived for a few years after my divorce was torn down. All these enormous changes catapulted me into quite an emotional state. I've been feeling a little lost—like I'm being erased. Everything is going away.

So, I turned to meditation to help me refocus. During meditation, Chase immediately jumped into the octahedron I created, and he put his arm around me. I put my head on his shoulder, and he said, "Hold on!" Before I knew it, we were on a roller coaster going up an enormous hill in the most glorious pink sunset. We rocketed down the hill and around turns and bolted through a loop while he raised his arms and screamed. I couldn't help but laugh and enjoy it, but I had to ask him why. Why were we doing this? Pretty soon all the other why questions started coming back. Why aren't you here? Why did you have to leave me? Why do I have to be alone? He said, "Mom, when we were on the roller coaster, did you worry about why we weren't still climbing up the hill or why we weren't at the top of the next hill? No! You wanted to get to the thrilling turns and twists and loops. Be grateful for the hill, because that was fun, but enjoy the stuff that is coming. It will be fun, too! Stop worrying about where you've been and what is over and enjoy what you have now and look forward."

So, I have been trying to be present and stop focusing on the past. When I attended Kevin's wedding, as Chase's closest friends lined up along the altar in the bridal party, I was moved to tears. I could feel that big gaping hole where he should have been. But, Chase immediately showed me that he was there. He wasn't missing at all. I don't have to like that he isn't here physically, but I get to know that he *is* here energetically. I can still have conversations and see him and feel him. He can guide me and advise me, which is an interesting turn of events for the parent to be guided by the child instead of vice versa! However, I will continue to seek his guidance as he knows far more than I do, and I've been able to learn from him every day as life continually changes and brings new and exciting challenges. It's so much easier to face them knowing I have a group of advisors to tap into whenever I choose to open that line of communication. The best part is that *anyone can do this*, and I hope that I can help others find their way to tap in and heal while I continue to do so myself.

Kim

I have always loved animals, so it was a natural progression from connecting to Dan to wanting to connect with animals. I remember seeing a bird outside my window nearly every day for several months. It would just look in the window, look at me, and then fly off. It was somehow very comforting to have it check in on me. I don't know if it was Dan incognito or he encouraged some nearby bird that I had never seen to come by for a few months, but I'm so glad it happened. I needed the consistency of its arrival to lean on, and for me, nature and animals have always felt more reliable than people. It was the perfect messenger of hope.

The first thing I decided to try was to learn about animal communication. I signed up for an online class. The class was only partially successful, not because of the teaching or method, but because in hindsight, I see that it was too soon. It was only six months after Dan had passed and the grief and shock that still hung over me made it difficult for me to be open to receiving messages from the animals. When I started the class, I was still working as a manager with a lot of responsibility, and I was trying to learn this very new skill on my lunch hour. It was difficult to turn off the thinking and action duties of reports and budgets to jump to the feeling, sensing, and being of animal communication, and then jump back again at the end of the hour. I was straddling two worlds all the time, and it was confusing and unsettling. But when practicing with the group, I did on occasion connect to the animal in the exercise for our group. One time, we were trying to connect and find a lost cat that belonged to someone in the class. When I connected to the cat, I felt everything the cat was feeling. I felt incredible sadness, loneliness, and confusion. I sat on the floor of Dan's office and sobbed uncontrollably. This experience shocked me, but the sobbing shut off as abruptly at it started at the end of my connection. I have since learned that I am an empath, which means I often feel what others are feeling. I knew if I was going to continue to practice this skill, I would need to figure out how to manage my human emotions.

Other things happened after I started learning to communicate with animals. Various animals that I did not know started to show up in my head at random times. It was if I had an "open for business" sign in the energy cosmos once I had set an intention to learn to communicate with them. One time I was in savasana at the end of my yoga class, and a dog I had never seen before popped in. I had to explain to it that I was busy now and asked it to come back later. This also happened occasionally when I was extra relaxed right before nodding off to sleep at night. But it was unclear to me at the time what I was supposed to do with these animals because I had no idea who they were or why they were showing up. I have since learned that I need to ask them. Other things happened as well. One day I was in my backyard and looked up to see a group of geese flying overhead. Without thinking, I said hello to them out loud and they turned to change their direction and fly directly over me. Another time, I was staying at a campground in the mountains. The owner told me that she was concerned because the lock on the garbage had been left open the night before and a bear and her cubs had gotten into the trash. Her concern was that bears often continued to come back once they had successfully gotten into the trash. That night, I decided to try to help the mama bear understand that teaching her cubs to get trash in a human campground was not in their best interest. I sat very still, shut my eyes, and talked quietly out loud to her. She wasn't there at the time, but I have learned that when I talk out loud, I am sending the message telepathically, which I believe helps the animals to understand. I just explained that although it seemed like easy food, teaching them to come near humans would not be good for them in the future. The next morning, I asked the owner if the bears had come back and she said, surprisingly, no.

In addition to the distractions from my job and my grief when I was trying to learn animal communication, in general, it seemed to be much harder for me to learn than healing. In fact, it seemed that the harder I tried, the less success I had. Dan explained that healing was my primary calling and that animal communication was a secondary role for me so I would have to work a little harder at it. So, I quit the animal communication course before finishing it and focused on learning about Reiki, crystals, and flower essences. In fact, at one point, Dan suggested I start an online business selling some kind of flower essence. I thought that was the most absurd thing I had ever heard, and it made me tired just thinking about starting a business. I was still fogged over with grief, just beginning to learn about energy healing and exhausted looking around our house trying to decide what to do next. But he was just tossing out ideas for me to do something that would allow me to step more firmly into my new world and provide income so I could stay in our house if I chose to do that. Needless to say, that did not appeal to me, so I sold our house instead. Although that solution did not feel appealing, I couldn't get enough of learning about energy and healing, and it all came very naturally to me. It was like breathing. While both of my dogs were interested in what I was doing, Bella was especially interested. Every time I was learning about energy healing, she became a willing participant if I needed to practice. She was excited about my new path, and it helped us bond and heal together. Once I left my job, I had less stress and more time and strength to explore energy work further. As my grief began to heal, the frequency and strength of my gift began to grow at a faster pace. And the truth is, I would never have found the path to my true purpose if Dan hadn't left. He said he is sorry I had to wait to do this work. But I know that part of what prepared me to do this work was our life together and my life experiences before that. My Chinese Medicine Practitioner had been telling me since Dan passed that the Universe was waiting for me to own this new path. I'm happy to say that I finally have. I read somewhere that sometimes you have to lose your life before you can find it. I know that was true for me. It wasn't easy to lose Dan, but finding him again allowed me to come out of the other side of grief whole, happy, and hopeful.

Sarina

With J.T. by my side, I felt I could face anything. Then, his angelversary hit. The "angelversary" is the anniversary of his passing, March 30th. I was full steam ahead with my continued training with J.T. and my other Master Teachers that were with J.T. They were teaching me so much about how to bring this information and training to others. I studied hard, meditated frequently, and journaled extensively. I still had to face and process the immense loss of burying my son, though. Those first two angelversaries were brutal. I was still grieving the loss of my physical child, my first born. At the same time, I was developing this out-of-this-world, new relationship with him, understanding where he was, why he left, what my part was in his leaving, and what I needed to do to fully step into my purpose.

There were times when I felt I could easily just slip away into his world. It was a beautiful place that words cannot describe. The colors are so vibrant, and the feelings so intense. It is everything I had dreamed of when contemplating "heaven." I would never leave by my own hand, but staying longer in meditation with him, being in that higher frequency space, was so much more pleasant than having to be in my body and suffer the pain of not having him here. J.T. would tell me, "Mom, you are in a body for a reason. You wanted to experience the denseness, as well as the crispness, of life on earth. You said you would help others find their own 'heaven.'" These were the times I wished I could send him to his room, put him on time-out for being a smart aleck to his mom. I couldn't argue with his logic, though. After extensive research into my own past lives and who I was on the other side, I knew he was right. So I sat in my grief, waiting. Waiting for it to swallow me into nothingness. But, just when I thought I couldn't take any more, I would feel a hand reach down and lift me out of the cesspool of grief. I was never alone, and I was always loved.

There were many who didn't understand that even though I could talk with my son, and I knew where he was, that I still had to go through what every other mother who loses a child goes through. "Oh, you are so lucky. You don't have to grieve because you have J.T. with you still," they'd say. I'd reply, "No. There is no 'get out of jail free' card for grief. We all have to go through it." They would look at me puzzled. How do you explain the dichotomy of these two worlds? I am still very much a human mom, even though I am also a medium and have connection with my son. I learned these two polarities can coexist. Just as feeling overwhelming sadness and happiness at the same time is possible. Whenever J.T. would bring me his "doppelgangers," those beautiful children who looked just like him here on the physical plane, a pain would go through my heart like no other, yet at the same time, I was so happy to "see" my boy again. I was living in a world of polarized ideas, concepts, realities and truths. Through it all, though, I had J.T. right there, helping me to understand the concepts and assimilate the information. And, boy, was there a lot of information. I knew I had to spend time in my grief, yet still stay focused to understand my new role as a spiritual teacher and healer.

Every day, J.T. and I would have "training sessions." He would teach me about where he was and the energy in that space. He taught me about creation, and showed me how we all create our world as we move through it. He also gave me new tools, so many new tools. He would give me a new tool, such as an easier way to transport to other places in the Universe, and I would be so overwhelmed, I would have to stop our work and go do something mundane, like clean my toilets, something to remind me I was still human. I felt so not human sometimes. My soul's growth was blasting into the stratosphere, yet the "me" that inhabited a very limited physical body still had to drive to the store to get eggs, or drive my children to their playdates and activities. I had to straddle the worlds, one foot in each, to keep grounded "here" on earth, and learn "there," in those other places.

There's no doubt I was not always successful in the delicate balancing act of being here and there. I'd forget appointments, to put gas in the car, to pay my bills on time. Being a very organized person, this drove me crazy. The end result was putting everything, even the smallest task, onto lists and on the calendar. I was very thankful for those Franklin-Covey classes I took when I was in corporate America way back when. I called on the "Sarina" from that time, those engineering days, to help me stay grounded and focused on my "3D" activities, while calling on my soul self to keep me connected to those other places.

Through all of this, I was still grieving. And healing. Every knife in the heart was an opportunity to move through a little more of the grief. They say it never ends, that you never are the same after losing a child. I somewhat agree with this statement, but resented being told by almost every other mother out there that my life was over. I would never find happiness again. I knew in my heart there was a better way. I knew from the beginning, I would be able to find a way to turn this around and help others. I had no idea in those early days to what extent. I continued following J.T. and all of my Master Teachers on the other side, learning, studying, meditating, and exploring. Initially, the years moved very slowly with constant reminders of my loss. At some point, time sped up, and suddenly I was five years out, ten years out, fifteen years out from J.T.'s transition. I attribute this time movement to the incredible work I was doing with J.T. He would present new projects to me, new classes to teach, and new events to attend. And more books to write! We were on the fast track, and neither one of us was going to be slowing down anytime soon. I'd say, "What do you want me to do next? What new tool do you have for me?" He'd reply, "I'm so glad you asked!"

Chapter Five
Now

Vickie

Justin was a member of the US Marine Corps Special Operations. While you might expect someone in that position to be boastful, Justin spoke very little of his "job." He kept his military life very separate from his family and friends. I knew that he was either training or deployed, but I knew little else. Whenever I tried to have a more specific discussion (what are you doing, what is your job?), his 6'2" frame would tap me on the top of the head and tell me, "That's really not for Moms to know." That would infuriate me. And I worried. Justin would speak of the men on his team, but only by their first names—and many of those were nicknames. I did not know them, or their families, and did not understand the bond they shared.

When Justin was killed in action, his military family became our family. They generously shared their stories of training, deployments, and of their teammate they had loved and lost. As a result, we had a clearer vision of the man Justin became after he left home. We shared a loss in common, and I felt they understood more about my loss than the average person. This unique, common ground we shared led me to seek others within my community who might also understand.

I began searching for a way to stay connected with the military community that had been so supportive. In addition to the ceremonies, events and fundraisers that honored Justin, I found a few local organizations that represented and supported various aspects of the military. It was through these activities that I learned of a local horse ranch offering equine therapy to veterans. It is a facility administered and run entirely by volunteers. I read studies of the documented success of equine therapy in treating PTSD, traumas, and other stress disorders. It was while volunteering at the ranch that I began to witness the working relationship between the horse and human.

My childhood was spent on a small farm in a rural community, and my grandparents lived very close to us. My grandfather was a horseman, and he was more than eager to share his love of horses with me. I received my first horse, a Shetland pony named Gypsy, for my fifth birthday. Our herd expanded over the years, and I eventually partnered with an Appaloosa gelding named Cherokee. I spent hours in the barn, playing, grooming the horses, or simply sitting on their backs while they munched happily on hay or grazed in the pasture. As I grew older, my horse became my primary mode of transportation. He took me to my grandparents, to the neighbors, or to visit my friends. Once I was old enough, I joined a 4-H group, learned to ride in the show ring, and competed in a few local shows. My childhood memories are of long summer days on the back of my horse.

Cherokee also became my best companion and confidant when emotions in my home grew tense. When those situations arose, I was able to escape to the barn or go out for a ride. Cherokee provided me with an emotionally safe zone to just "be." Any situation became more manageable after time spent with my horse.

I began volunteering at the equine-therapy ranch mucking stalls and feeding the herd. I was elated to be back in my emotional safe zone. Just being back in a barn was so soothing. A couple of years passed, and a high school friend offered me two horses of my own. What began as an amazing experience volunteering at the ranch led me to having two of my own horses with whom I bonded immediately. The amount of healing that resulted from this connection was astounding.

I participated in an equine-assisted therapy program because I wanted to look deeper into the horse-human connection. I found that a horse will join with a person that matches their own energy. As an example, I watched a very timid mare shy away from an extremely anxious, somewhat stern, young man. As the weeks went by, the young man was able to identify what he was feeling. As a result, he was also able to lower his energy and be present. In the sessions that followed, the same mare became quite comfortable with this young man, and even walked directly to him on her own.

I have read scientific studies showing that the horse's energy fields are five times larger than humans, with the strongest energy radiating from their heart. These studies confirmed what I had felt as a child—that the horse holds space to allow for healing so we can discover whatever we are not yet seeing in ourselves. The horse in the wild is preyed upon and must constantly be aware of its surroundings to survive. The horse does not worry about what happened yesterday, or what might happen tomorrow, but is focused on the present. Attempting to interact with the horse while your mind is racing about the events of the day or what might happen tomorrow is difficult. To have any success with the horse, you must learn to speak their language by being fully present and aware of your surroundings.

Having to face Justin's loss has brought me to this path. I would never have wished to be here without my son and would give anything to have him here. I also understand that this is all part of our plan, and I am so grateful for Justin's persistence and constant presence while guiding me here.

My childhood connection with Cherokee was the precursor to Horse becoming essential in my own personal healing and in my work to help others. Energetically, I was led to mediumship, animal communication and Reiki training. With Justin's guidance, and the beautiful heart energy of Horse, we connect intuitively in an energetically safe space for self-discovery. I continue to receive mentoring and training in these areas so that I might also share this healing space with others on their own path to self-discovery. I share my experiences with others to offer an example of the value of authenticity, and the intention of offering comfort, healing and growth.

Carrie

I am still very early in the development of my abilities to communicate, and I am working hard to trust my intuition and instincts. Often, I feel very sure during the moment when I am communicating with Spirit, but afterwards I get a sort of imposter syndrome when time has passed, and I allow myself to question what I've heard or learned. Constant validation from my son has helped with this issue, and I'm learning every day to trust myself more. I am practicing the ability to connect with Spirit more deeply and with more ease.

I am also just trying to adjust to letting my son take the lead and guide me through the healing and learning process. It sure is a challenge to hand the reins over to my child, but he is the one with more experience and knowledge now! Slowly, but surely, he is helping me heal my grief and come to terms with his absence in the physical world. There is always this battle between my heart that misses his physical presence here and the knowledge deep in my soul that he hasn't truly left. I have moments where I feel that I have completely accepted this new role in life (or at least I really try to), and then the waves of grief blow me over because I mourn him and the earthly milestones he won't achieve. Yet, Chase always makes his presence known and turns it around so that I am reminded that he isn't really gone, and he shows me that we are both exactly where we need to be!

Currently, there is an interesting transition brewing in my life right now, as my only other child, my daughter Sadie, has truly flown the nest. It has been a bit of a prolonged process getting here because Chase's loss kept her close (or at least my need for her after his loss) and, fortunately, the college she attended was only a short drive away. Then, the COVID lockdown brought her home while she studied remotely for an extended time, which was an unexpected gift. Now, she has recently graduated medical school, married, and moved out of state to begin her residency program. As a single mother, Sadie has been my focus, and this has been an extremely busy year to support her through all these huge life events. Now that she is settling into her new life, my transition into a true "empty nester" has begun. Any bereaved parent knows that all those big life events bring on a tsunami of grief. But, Chase is here with me helping me to sort out my path, and he has stirred up some excitement for the adventure that we are about to begin. I'm not exactly sure what all he has in store for me, but he has been extremely present, and I can't go five minutes without someone mentioning his name, or a memory, or hearing his songs. He is sending so many signs—it's the spiritual equivalent of "Mom. Mom. Hey, Mom!"

Chase has been showing me a bit of what he is doing, as his soul continues to still have a purpose and a job to perform, even on the other side. In life, he was a protector and did what he could to help others get what they needed for their mental and physical health. There have been so many friends who told me that Chase helped them seek out a counselor for anger management or to end the cycle of self-harm. He would attend appointments with them to offer support, and he was sure to be there for them when they needed a friend afterward. Once, he talked to some boys in his dorm who had not acted appropriately with one of his female friends. He was peaceful, but he made his point that their actions would not be tolerated. He used his massive size and his big heart to make sure everyone around him felt safe.

His work to take care of others has continued. He has been working with other family members and friends here on the earthly plane, and he is helping those who have passed. He has a large network of young friends with him in the spiritual world. He was greeted by some of these friends when he crossed, and now he is doing the same for others. As I've mentioned earlier, he guided my niece in crossing over. To help soften this blow to my deeply grief-stricken family, he let some family members know that she was with him and that she is fine now. He is helping his friends here, as well. He works with them through dreams, songs on the radio, and gentle nudges of thought. Many of these people aren't terribly aware that Chase is behind their inspiration and the answers that appear, but he is in the background supporting them. He is still watching over the people he loves but in a much more subtle way.

With me, he is being a lot less subtle. With all the transition going on in my world, there is a massive clearing happening. After Chase passed, I could not stand to be home alone for more than two days at a time. In the summer, I had to find summer jobs to keep my mind busy, so that I wouldn't let my grief overwhelm me. I had moments when I truly didn't know if I'd be able to survive, and I honestly feared what I might do in the extreme pain I was feeling. In that space of seven years, I filled my time like a person filling the kitchen junk drawer. I took classes, participated in numerous training courses, joined committees, and took on extra duties at work. I tutored students during after school hours, I volunteered to babysit, and I did anything I could do to fill up every single second of my time. Naturally, this constant mental and physical chaos has made connecting to Spirit very difficult.

So, as life and Chase have cleared my schedule, Chase is letting me know that there are some new plans for me. I do know that more meditation is on the agenda. Clearing space in the house for a dedicated area to meditate and setting a dedicated schedule to meditate is a must. He is steering me to take some courses in Reiki and to develop and strengthen my skills in mediumship. There is also the likelihood that my career will need to change to line up a bit more with some of these new ventures, so additional schooling is also something that will likely happen. I firmly feel that I am being led to a career as a counselor, and it seems that may be the correct path for me. Luckily, I have always said that I am a lifelong learner and I love school…I just never imagined that my ultimate teacher would be my son.

Kim

I signed up for an animal Reiki class with Sarina very soon after Dan passed. Both dogs were mourning his loss, and I was desperate to make them feel better, which, in turn, might make me feel better. From the beginning, I was led to learn energy healing to help animals. I learned it quickly and started practicing it with my dogs, who seemed to really enjoy the positive vibration it brought into our lives. I liked Reiki because I could feel the energy buzzing in my hands, giving me proof that it was there, that it was real. And because it wasn't me doing anything other than calling it in, I couldn't mess it up, and it always made things better. The room in our house that I stayed in for months became saturated with grief, anger, and confusion. Sarina, who taught me Reiki, suggested that I use my newfound skills to clear the energy in the room, and it worked. Sometimes I used the Reiki energy on myself, if I had a headache or a stomachache, and it worked. Later, I signed up to learn more advanced levels of Reiki, but I kept falling back to what I learned in the animal Reiki class and focusing on helping animals. I only used my new skills occasionally when helping people I knew or their animals, but really didn't own my role as an animal healer until recently. I visited the Bahamas with an animal communicator and learned about dolphin energy, which I fumbled through and used to calm my stomach after days out on a boat, and it worked. During one of our evening educational circles, we each reached out to another person's pet at home. I struggled to connect with someone's cat. I asked him some questions, and he would answer, then he would disconnect. I would try again, using Reiki as a connecting tool this time, he would answer a few more questions and then disconnect. I managed to write down answers to about half of the questions on the worksheet before the owner said, "Yeah, he doesn't like to do this much." I sighed with relief and smiled to myself. It wasn't just me fumbling my way through; he didn't like to do this much. He was my lesson that you can't (and shouldn't) make animals participate if they don't want to. You invite them to join in, and wait for them to accept it or not. It was soon after this trip that my Dolphin spirit guide, Matilda, appeared during a meditation. She said she was going to help me find joy again. She did always make me smile when she was being silly and sassy, but I wasn't holding my breath for joy.

After I cleaned out and sold the house that Dan and I shared, I really began to let go of what was, and began to embrace what could be. The void that Dan (and our house) left in my life began to be filled with learning about other kinds of healing energy that could help animals, and animal communication began to resurface in my life. My two dogs were having some issues getting settled in the condo I rented and struggling over who would be "top dog" at the new place. For some reason, I have more trouble reading my own animals than other peoples' animals sometimes. It might be because I'm trying too hard again. But in any event, I contacted a professional animal communicator. We had to wait several months to get an appointment, and by the time we had our session, the reason I had made the appointment was mostly resolved. I decided to have the session anyway and just asked her to tell me what was on each of their minds. Both dogs were asleep on the couch until she connected with them, and then each in turn woke up and sat up. Bella was first and after talking about how she could more productively use her excess energy, her message to me was "she wished I would finish unpacking the boxes from the move so she could find her stuff." Butch, my older dog was next. When I asked if there was anything I could do for him to make his life better, he said "he would like to stay outside longer so he could sniff the grass" instead of coming right back inside after going potty. Needless to say, I had failed to pick up on both of those messages.

After I felt more healed, I began traveling to spend time with other kinds of animals and learn about their healing energy. I also wanted to hear what messages they had for me and humans in general. I knew from working with animal communicators that each kind of animal is unique in their gifts and lessons. I traveled with a small group of people and an animal communicator to visit the gray whales in Mexico. Gray whales teach us forgiveness, and with that comes a tremendous sense of peace. Next, I went to spend time with a herd of horses that have kept their wild nature. Those horses taught me transparency, strength, courage, and freedom along with confirming my call to send healing energy to horses. I have other trips planned to spend more time with whales and dolphins and to visit the white lions of South Africa. I feel so honored that animals want to share their healing energy and lessons with me. I made a vision board this year and wrote in big letters, "I am an animal healer." Since doing that, opportunities to help animals began to emerge.

Now

I am finally stepping fully into my purpose, and Dan (and the Universe) is cheering me on. I have started a business, Animals Feel Better, to provide healing energy to animals either in-person or remotely. I am committed to volunteering some of my services to animals who are rescued, in foster arrangements, are providing healing and therapeutic services to humans, or are in zoos or in the wild. I believe strongly in offering healing energy to animals and letting them use the energy in a way that they intuitively know how to do, if they so choose. The health and wellbeing of animals is a complex matter. But in my experience, sending positive, loving, respectful, healing energy helps support animals on their journey so they can do the work they came here to do. I am certified as a dolphin and whale healing energy practitioner with the intention of helping animals of all kinds feel better. My dog, Bella, loves this energy. My dog, Butch, who I was sure was leaving me at the end of last year, chose to stay another seven months and made a miraculous recovery so he could continue to watch my transformation. When he did finally cross over, he left with a commitment to help me reach dogs with anxiety, fear, or reluctance to try new things. It just doesn't get any better than this. The other day I had my calendar open and caught myself writing "I love my life!" at the top of the page. Ever since I found my lane and owned my place in this world, my health continues to improve, and I'm well on my way to the best chapter of my life. As soon as I let go of the attachment to what was, a whole new world of possibilities unfolded. I assure you that Dan is not gone. He has been here all along, pulling me kicking and screaming into this brand new, miraculous life. I couldn't have done it without him, and I'm so glad I didn't have to.

Sarina

I can't tell you where I would be if I hadn't found my son. I have no idea if I would have survived the loss. Despite getting up every morning for my two other children, the pain of losing a child is deeper than anything else I could have ever imagined. That is not to say others' grief was any less grueling than mine. I learned early in my career as a medium that loss is loss, whether it is a child, a beloved pet, a spouse, or a dear parent. Many would argue with me on this point, but it is my feeling that the heart-piercing pain of losing someone you love goes beyond all demographics, nationalities, ages, and circumstances.

I have made it my life's work to ease that heart-piercing pain, to bring closure to those left here, lost and confused. I have made it my life's work to teach others about how I found J.T. again, and what a simple process it was to stay connected and learn to receive from him. Though this process is "simple," it is not always "easy." Over the last fifteen years, I have learned how I still get in my own way sometimes. I don't see the picture J.T. and the Masters are trying to show me. I get caught up in what I call "3-D land," our three-dimensional world and the rules we are supposed to follow. Talking to dead people? Really? Traveling to other places in the Universe to learn new tools? Really? Bending time so I can finish a project by the deadline? Really?

I look back on my life prior to this incredible connection with J.T. and the Masters and wonder how I got as far as I did. How in the world did I not totally screw myself? J.T. reminds me, "We were always with you, guiding you in your life. Think back, Mom." In that moment, I remember countless times when I was guided. I was given tools to get out of terrible relationships. I was blessed with grace when I didn't listen, went my own way anyway, and learned via the two-by-four method, learning that I should have gone left at the fork instead of right. I've always felt loved, but it wasn't the love of this earthly place. It was love from an incredible force of energy. I was nurtured, protected, guided, and loved from beyond this world. I just never could put words to it or understand why.

Now, I know we are all loved like this. No exceptions. Regardless of what you have done, or not done, who you think you have hurt, what you have said, you are loved. So many of my clients can't possibly fathom this, given what they were told by those around them, and who they believe themselves to be. I can say, though, that one hundred percent of the time, they understand this when their session is done. They may not be ready to hear it depending on their relationship with the loved one who passed, but our loved ones and our incredible guides plant the seeds of love in every session.

Those loved ones on the other side with whom I connect during sessions also talk a lot about forgiveness. Forgiveness has a very weird energy on this planet. I hear people say, "Oh, I could never forgive that!" Or, "They could never forgive me for that!" I understand these concepts since we associate forgiveness with weakness so much of the time. If we forgive, then the other person wins, and we lose. This is not the case when we are talking about forgiveness from the other side. They see the big picture now. They see their part in whatever happened between us and them. There are always two sides to a situation, and when we transition into that other space, we are shown these situations from the other's point of view. We get to feel what they felt and see what they saw. This gives us a very different perspective on what was happening. If only we could see this perspective here! We would save ourselves so many years of separation if we could understand how the other person was seeing and experiencing the issue.

To be clear, it is not always about forgiveness. The term I hear more often from the other side is "release." They say we must release ourselves from the feelings of hurt, betrayal, and anger, as these energies are very low on the frequency scale and actually harm us energetically. Everything on our planet is energy. Plants are energy, water is energy, air is energy, and we are energy. When we hold onto anger, for example, our energetic frequency slows down. In this state of energy, we can block ourselves from experiencing the energy of love, joy, happiness, peacefulness, and abundance. So, holding onto this dense energy creates a cycle of lower frequency energy in our systems. It can cloud what is real, and the truth of the situation. Granted, we are human. We did come to experience all of the emotions, not just the "good" stuff. But we also came here to learn how to free ourselves from the heavy energies all around us, so we can be in purpose and in true relationship with others. We can't do this if we are in a state of low frequency. Remember, your soul came here to learn about love and relationships and to fulfill a purpose. Getting out of your own way by releasing those lower energy emotions can help you to move into the flow of your own life. When you are in the flow, life is more peaceful, fulfilling, and purposeful.

Our loved ones on the other side understand this is not a switch that happens overnight, and because of this, they offer their assistance, love, forgiveness, and strength to the loved ones still here in body. I, personally, am so appreciative of my loved ones' help, especially J.T. He gives me wisdom, light, understanding, and a perspective from where he is. More than all of this, though, he gives me love. A love that I have never experienced on our earthly plane. This love is true, unconditional, nurturing, and warm. It is that love that goes beyond anything we can comprehend with our limited cognitive functions. It is that love that we all remember from before we were born into these lives, and the love you read about from those who have experienced the other side and returned. The crispness, intensity, and texture of this love does not exist here, but the great news is, it does exist. It exists and is within reach for everyone, no exceptions.

I am blessed to be able to experience this love on a daily basis. I invite you to jump into the deep end with me and experience it for yourself. Simply ask for your loved one to be with you right now, and to shower you with that love. You are deserving of this love. You are part of this love. And this love is already a part of you. Relax and receive. You are loved.

Epilogue
In Their Own Words

Justin

You might be sad and feel that we are no longer at your side. We know that the grief of our loss is real, and it's hard, and we understand. What you are feeling—what you are living—that's hard stuff. Please don't be sad that we are no longer there, and please don't worry. We have it pretty darn easy here. Let me tell you, this place is amazing! Think of the pictures you see of the Garden of Eden, only on steroids. The colors are so vibrant, and so beautiful—the flowers, the colors, every sunrise, every cloud, every sunset, the birds, and, oh man, the horses! It's a magical place to be.

The energy is so clear and soothing. It's like the way you feel on the top of a mountain. It is the best view, and you can see for miles and miles. Go there and look at the vastness of it all. I know you can feel it.

Understand that there is a reason we are here, and it's to help you with your work on Earth. Please know that we are here to help you, to guide you, and to protect you.

There is a group of guys with me. Most of us served together, but not all. We are all leaders, each one of us. We are also very high energy. Many of these guys left like me, but not all of them have left. Some are still physically there with you. We watch over our families, and we are all working to help our brothers still in the fight. We are with them for the day-to-day, as well as to help them accomplish what they have sworn to do. We know what they are doing is tough. Deployments are tough. Our job is to make it easier, to let them know that they are not alone. We supported each other before we left, and we continue to do so now. We take this job even more seriously now—supporting our men—than when we were on Earth.

Our mission, always, is to send love to all of you. Love will make the world a better place. Yes, it is that simple, and yes, it is possible. If it were not possible, we would not be working so hard at it.

But we need your help, too. We need your help in raising the energy, and to bring joy. There are some that will not see or acknowledge this, but we want you to believe it anyway. Remember that love is the most powerful energy anywhere, and it is the one energy that connects us all. We are making that happen. Love is what brought my mom along on this adventure, her love for me. She feels my love for her, and it comforts her. It helps others also. Love is where it's at.

My mom has worked so hard to communicate with me. She brought herself up out of despair, which means she had to raise her energy, so that she could connect with me. That's big. And her work is a great example to show you all how this is possible. It did not come easily for her, but she is committed to it because she wants us to continue to be together. I want you to know that you can do this, too.

We want to talk to you and help you in this life. It is our job and desire for you to succeed. In my earth life, I wanted a goal, worked at it, and pushed everyone along with me so that we could succeed together. Now, I can join you for the ride and help you arrive at your goals. Love, the world needs love, and you can spread it as far as the eye can see. My team will be there for you. The view is so crazy here. We can see you, and we see you struggle and take the wrong path, and we try to say, "Hey! Not that way!" But it is up to you to choose the path that is right for you. If you listen, you can hear us cheering you on. You can connect with your loved ones over here. Believe that you can, seek guidance, and know we are here waiting. Keep trying, keep connecting. Don't give up. Keep working at it because we are all here waiting for you, and when you get here, we will continue our work.

When I was there, I used to tell my mom that whatever physical pain she had was, "all in your head." I told her that the pain was not real, and it only existed in her head. She would argue with me, identifying the specific muscle that was painful. Now I'm telling you to get out of your head. I want you to feel, to trust your gut, and to follow your dreams. We're here to help with that, too. We want you to succeed.

I wanted my mom to participate in this book, obviously. She wants to work with you in your healing, and she has accepted the gift from Horse. She is working on a way to share this gift with all of you. That beautiful Horse heart energy will surround you, lift you, and embrace you. And I will be there helping, too. Not to help with Horse; they don't need my help. We want you to know how much you are loved, and the beautiful Horse energy will help with that.

Remember, love comes first. If you can remember that, then the other details will not matter. Just allow the love to come in. Breathe, connect, and repeat. Go out into the world and share this with others, and by "share," we mean to live your life with meaning. Those who are ready will follow and join. Others may not be ready, and that's okay. You must keep going. Don't you quit!

We are here for all of you. We understand that you have free will and may not accept our help, but we want you to know that it is here. I am here. Simply call on us for assistance, and remember, it's all about love.

Chase

You know this. You know what I have to say. Love is all that matters. Keep the conversation going with us, even though we know it is hard for you. There are so many benefits for us to keep communicating. It may feel very strange and very different, but it is still communication, and it is still love. All you should ever worry about is love—are you giving love? Are you loving each other and loving yourself? That is the only thing that matters. You can get so caught up in your everyday tasks and work and misery. Go out and live more and enjoy nature and each other. Nothing else is that big of a deal!

Look at us! We are here and we are whole. You can feel us. You can see us, and we are more whole here than we ever were down there. We are more *this* (referring to his current state of energy) during our existence than we will ever be in your physical state. This is our natural existence. My mom thinks of our time here as a trip we are taking together, and some of us leave the trip earlier than others. That couldn't be more accurate. I was on the trip for 21 years, and I left to head on a different journey. It's as if we can still text and call while we are on our separate trips. We are just not physically on your trip with you. We can enjoy it through you and with you as we hear your stories and watch you. This is a far better way to observe and share it with you than just seeing pictures on Facebook or Instagram! If we were on vacation and I left earlier than you, would you spend the rest of your vacation not enjoying yourself because I left for my own trip? You might be a little bummed out, and, of course, you would miss how much fun I add to it, but you could still find things to enjoy and do. Do that. Stop grieving those of us who head out on another trip! You are wasting your time!

Don't waste your time! Go on adventures! Get together with people. Have happy gatherings with people laughing and having a good time. That raises your vibration. That is what you are here for—to have fun, explore, laugh, and do things you enjoy with people you enjoy. My mom just watched a video clip of Matthew McConaughey that said he asked his kid what he wanted to learn from going to summer camp, and his kid said, "I just want to meet new people and do cool things." That's it. That's why you are here: to meet new people and do cool things. Live while you're here. That is very important. People get caught up in life sometimes—the making of a life, and you forget to enjoy life and do what makes you feel alive and passionate. Don't let making a living bog you down. Ask for help with that. We can help you.

Even when we die and we are in this energetic state, we love you. We still love you. We always love you, and we know you love us. We're all okay. That is what you need to remember and to know. We will always be fine, and you will be fine. We acknowledge the difficulty for you, but don't spend too much time there. Spend very little time there. That doesn't get you closer to us. Exploration, fun, laughter—that gets you closer to us. You need higher vibrations. Do what you can in love, for love, with love.

People need to know they can reach their loved ones. *Anyone* can do this. It may take a while and feel weird, and you may question the information you get (and your sanity), but anyone can do this. And you should! We want to offer guidance and still be a part of your lives. Not in the make-a-shrine-of-the-dead's-personal-items way (*that was for Carrie's benefit*), but as a real relationship with a person like you would have on Earth. Talk to us. Ask us questions. Open yourself up to guidance. Ask us what we have to say. We are here. We want to communicate. People need to know that, more than likely, their loved ones are trying to get their attention!

We know you are worried about spending too much of your time with us here and forgetting to live. We will help you with that. That can't be the reason not to meditate and reach us. We won't allow you to spend all of your time here. We will give you what you need.

Fear keeps you from living so much. So many blocks in life are just fear. Take time to recognize when it is fear. There is nothing to fear. We are always here, and we love you. *We* can help you if you want to be helped.

Physical pain can be helped. Ask us to help. Don't let physical pain stop you from living life. Choose to be well.

People need to know that addiction can be helped. We can help with that. The hard part is that the person who is addicted may not be ready to ask for help. Those who love that person can ask, however. That will help guide the addicted person, but it is ultimately their choice to ask. We can help guide them to that.

That is all anyone needs to know. We're all here, generations waiting for you, helping you. *We* love you.

Dan

You each have a special gift that is unique to you. You don't have to wait until you are faced with a challenge to grab onto it. For Kim, it is her love of animals. Animals bring her joy and actually helping them feels even better. For you, it may be something different. Learn how to slow down, be still, and listen for what is calling to you. Lean into and embrace what comes to mind and see how it makes you feel. If thinking of it brings you joy, you are on the right track. For many people, the busyness of their daily lives drowns out what their inner voice is trying to tell them. What makes your heart sing? Each person has something special that allows them to bring their unique qualities to their calling and do it in a way that only they can do it. Kim's Chinese Medicine practitioner had been telling her for years that the Universe was waiting for her to embrace her role as an animal healer or, as Kim would say, to get in her lane. Once she did, everything changed. Don't discount the power you have to change everything. When you are in human form, you tend to see only limitations. But from here, all I see is vast possibilities. After I left, I told Kim to meditate and write. She did the writing, which helped her heal and led to her story in this book. But it wasn't until she started meditating that she was still enough to see the real reason she is here. Meditation leads to seeing things as they could be, or as they are already deep inside you. Anything is possible if you close your eyes, stop doing, and just be in the moment. Then, take one tiny step toward what you see, and watch and see how things begin to change.

At first, you might get bogged down in the details like how to do what you are being called to do. Don't worry about that. It will all work itself out once you grab on to what is calling to you. Whatever it is that brings you joy, just start doing it! Like Kim, you may not be able to dive in full-time right away, but do it anyway. Take it out for a test drive. Dip your big toe in the water of your dream and see how it feels. If it feels like I think it's going to feel, pretty soon you won't be able to *not* do it. For Kim, when she first started learning animal communication, it was too soon after I transitioned. As much as I wanted to "will" her down the road of grief, she had to travel at her own speed. But once she tried out her newfound gift, she kept coming back to it again and again. Now animal communication is becoming an integral part of her work as an animal healer. Once you know what lights you up and you embrace it, learn more about it, and find others who love it as much as you do. Look for teachers and mentors, books and podcasts, and wherever else you can find information. Learn everything you can at first, and then keep what resonates with you, and give gratitude for the rest and let it go. Build yourself a team of like-minded supporters. Learn from each other, help each other, and travel down the road of discovery together. Kim will tell you that she is an introvert, but even she needed people to help and support her. The momentum of her progress really began to speed up after she connected with her team of new friends. It can be tough to find and travel a new path on your own. The good news is that you don't have to.

One of the most important things for you to do is to reconnect yourself with the earth. You may have heard of being "grounded." Well, this takes it to a whole new level. Sit in meditation and ground yourself deep into the earth. Next, feel your connection up and outward to the moon and the stars. Doing this will help you feel part of something bigger. It will help you think BIG and dream BIG, bigger than you could ever have imagined. Feeling your connection to the Source of everything (some might call that God or Creator) will give you the energy you need to live your purpose. Imagine what the Universe is telling you to do based on the reason that you came to this lifetime. If you are living your life's purpose, how can you fail? The only way you can fail is passively choosing to not discover and live the life that you were meant to live. I promise you that when you discover what that life is, the Universe will applaud. You and everything else will be in perfect sync. You will feel as if time has stopped and notice nothing else around you. You will declare, just as Kim did, *that you love your life!* I know that it isn't easy, but it will be so worth it when you do it. I remember the human struggles of relationships, health concerns, and so many other things that might get in the way of you living the life that you are meant to live. But that is the beauty of doing it anyway, despite the challenges. I think many humans, maybe even you, have wondered why you are on the earth. I promise you that there is an answer. But only you can discover it and grab onto it. I am dedicated to helping humans find their way through the emotion, the disappointment, and the struggle to find something better, something greater than you can possibly imagine. I know it's not easy, but it will be worth it. I promise.

Take it one step at a time. Find your bearings and start again. Just keep putting one foot in front of the other toward what you imagine. If you get stuck, ask for help. There are so many of us waiting for you to ask for help and guidance. Call in loved ones who have passed, your guides, your angels, or me. I loved the day Kim quit trying to figure out who exactly was the best one to ask for help and said, "Whoever can help me with this situation, I could really use some help. Thank you." Every time she does that, someone always shows up to help her. Sometimes it's me, sometimes not, but the best possible help always shows up. All you have to do is believe that we are here and ask for help when you need it. And don't forget to breathe. Your breath is one of the easiest ways to connect to your higher self or to connect you with others. Then wait for something to happen. Something might get easier, information you need may show up, or someone may show up to support you. Nothing in the Universe is an accident. There are no coincidences.

So, what are you waiting for? We are here, cheering you on. We are so proud of you for choosing your authentic path and doing what you came to earth to do.

J.T.

You are a very important soul. You have chosen to be witness to the incredible energy changes on our planet. Even more, your high-frequency soul wants to be an active participant in this change. You said, "Yes! I want to be a part of this! I want to help the energy of *all that is* by incarnating once again at this special time! I am ready!"

Now, you must be saying to yourself, "Really? What in the world was I thinking?!" And the truth is, that is exactly what you were thinking—"How do I help the world?"

We have done this "world" thing for quite some time now. We've gone through different iterations and scenarios. We have come together as a species and made better decisions for our futures. We have also totally obliterated our hard work and blown the whole thing up in our faces.

We hear you say, "What? It was worse than it is now??" Yes, it was. As crazy as the world appears right now, imagine it with much more chaos and confusion. You see, there is evolvement and enlightenment. You as a whole are in higher frequency than your predecessors. You know more. You learn more. You respond more. You are working more than ever to be who you are as a soul, to embody that light in the denseness of your incarnation.

The chaos in the earth's current iteration is part of the experience. And, yes, you, the high-frequency soul, is excited to be here, part of the tearing down and rebuilding, once again, of the structures that no longer work for our energetic frequencies.

You must understand this before the real work can be done.

There is a myth among humans that if you are evolved and enlightened, you will not experience the chaos and confusion of the world around you. But you are different. Your soul understands the mission and also understands that just because you are in high frequency, it doesn't mean life will be perfect. You will still have lessons to understand and experience. There is a myth that once you are enlightened, there is no more pain and suffering. We can say that once you are enlightened, you understand the pain and suffering. You understand the origins from which you came, and you understand why you are enduring the pain and suffering. You are also given a choice on this: to continue to learn or to let it go. But enlightenment does not mean lighter than air and without a body. You still have work to do, and your soul wants the experience. Your higher self is here with you and supports you in your incarnations and in the incredible work you are doing. You are very special, and you must understand that this road is not for the faint of heart, or the ones who are not able to adapt and learn. No, you have shown time and time again how adaptable you are and how you are able to listen with your heart, tuning into your fellow human, and bringing light to those around you. There is so much more for you now. Right now.

We are entering a new phase of energy, and we want you to partake in the shift. We want you to be part of the energy flow. You already have the tools you need. The time is now to change who you are and where you are, so you are in alignment with this new energy. This is especially important if you have energy around you that is holding you back from being the bright star you are. We are not saying to remove those people, but we are saying there has to be some discernment in where you put your energy and where you put your focus. I would like to help you understand your bright light. I see your place in this new energy flow, and I invite you to see what I see. If you would like to come along, we have some steps for you to consider.

The first step is to understand who you are and the voice you have in your soul. This is a very important aspect of your energy. Sound is frequency, so using your voice helps with frequency. It also allows us to help you. Using your sound will take you to the place of connection with the Universe. This special frequency is the frequency of Om.

The frequency of Om vibrates within the heart, which is the center of your energetic being. Use different pitches of Om to feel which is best for you. This is not complicated or difficult to achieve. Use your heart to guide you.

Connect with Om every morning and every night, even if it is only for a minute. This will tune your frequency to be in alignment with the Universe. This is Step One.

Step Two is to accept who you are, and who you are not. You are a high-frequency soul with a mission and a purpose. You are not a victim of circumstance, or at the will of the river's current, carrying you where it wants you to go. At any time on this ride, you can redirect your reality and change the current. Understand you are so much more powerful than your mind can imagine. But your heart knows. Remember, the heart is the center of your energetic being. Your heart knows the magnitude of your energy. Accept the enormity of your soul.

Step Three is move energy out of your space that is holding you back or limiting you. Again, we understand there are physical limitations in your incarnation. After all, it's part of the human experience. There are other limitations, though, which you have accepted as your own, but they are not. These limitations do not come from your soul. They come from outside of you. These could be what your parents told you, or your teachers, or others in your life to whom you gave your power. This is not a criticism at all. Part of the human experience is to experiment with new thoughts and feelings. Sometimes you take these from others because they have told you they belong to you. Sometimes you take these thoughts and feelings because it is what you are expected to do. In any case, you may find they do not fit you. This is where you are able to take back your power and your energy. Let the Universe know you are ready to get rid of what is not yours. Make the statement now that it is time to step into your trueness and your beauty. Ask us to help move that old energy out to prepare for the new.

Step Four is to be big. This can be a challenge for many, as you were taught to believe that being big meant you were being egocentric or self-centered. We want you to think of this differently now. Your soul wants to learn all it can in this incarnation and to truly step into your Divine self, who you came here to be. Your soul does not want you to be small. Practice looking in the mirror each day and telling your reflection what a beautiful, powerful soul you are. Look into your eyes and see that fire, that Divine light. Tell yourself, "It's time. I'm ready!"

Step Five is to live as if you are already in the energy shift. Look around you. You are already here! Now, we just need to bring it into your reality. To do this, we ask that you live your life from that higher space. Look at others differently, through the lens of the new energy. Have patience with those still shifting. Everyone has their own pace. This includes being patient with yourself, too. You can be very critical of yourself, chastising yourself for not being where the "others" are yet. Remember, you are already in the energy. It is still working in your energetic system to bring your incarnation to its frequency.

Accept others for where they are. There is no need to preach. They are exactly where they need to be.

Look inward, not outward. Use your own heart and soul energy as your gauge. You do not need to look around to see where anyone else is. You are all on the same ride. I see it like a roller coaster. Some are still waiting in line to get on. Others are flying down the track. Others are climbing that crest right before that big drop. And others have finished the ride and are getting back in line to ride again! Everyone moves at his or her own pace through the ride. You are no different, and you should not expect yourself to be anywhere other than where you are right now. Your heart knows this. Your soul knows this.

So, as we embark on this new journey together, you and I are side by side. We know what we need to do. We have the tools to do it. And both of us have very important parts to play.

You are a very important soul. I see you. You are a star, so beautiful and bright. And I will be here to tell you this whenever you forget. We are a team, and we couldn't do this without you. Shine brightly, dear soul, and know your contribution to the collective is immeasurable!

Postscript
Writing This Book

Vickie

In nearly every meditation since Justin left, he encouraged me to write. I remember how he had kept a journal, and I thought that was what he wanted me to do. I have dozens of notebooks filled with my thoughts, daily experiences, gratitude, and loss. My journals became a vessel that carried the heavy weight of everything I felt uncomfortable sharing with others. It became my safe place.

I joined Sarina, Carrie and Kim in a writing workshop with the intention of organizing what I had been writing over the years. When the workshop grew into writing for this book, I was both excited and nervous. I wondered how my experiences could offer anything different than what any mother feels with this type of loss. Now that the book is complete, I realize the point in sharing is not so much my unique story, but in knowing that this connection is available to everyone. It is my hope that others facing this type of loss will find comfort in knowing that they are not alone.

Working with these ladies, and their shared energies, has been incredibly rewarding. I am forever grateful to each of them, and most grateful to my beautiful son—AKA Mr. Bossy Pants—for his guidance in making it happen.

Carrie

I cannot begin to express how grateful I am to Sarina for offering us this opportunity to learn how to connect to our spirit guides and write. I was thrilled to learn more about connecting to Spirit, and I could do it so much easier when I worked with Sarina. It never occurred to me when I registered for this class that it would result in a published product!

Writing this book was a much-needed push for me. This past year was my busiest professionally and personally, so the last thing I felt I could handle was adding one more task to the to-do list. Unfortunately, there were times when I let this experience feel like a task because I was so bogged down with work this year. However, the energy that this group of women brought to the project, as well as the dedicated time for focused meditation and writing, was exactly what I needed to follow through on getting a finished product worth sharing. Having our "co-authors" set deadlines caused me to panic, but without that push from them, I doubt that I would have ended up with an organized or completed piece of work.

It feels very bittersweet to come to the end of this project. As excited as I am to see how our work is received, the healing and connections I've made through working in this group have changed my life. I have evolved so much throughout this venture, and I am worried about interrupting the momentum that I've gained. Working with this group of women helped me to connect with my son and spirit guides with so much more clarity and intention. Every meeting we had together allowed me to learn more from my son and validate that what I was "getting" was accurate. It was also just as helpful to hear what the others were experiencing after they meditated and wrote, as it was for me to meditate and write. I am eager to see the finished product, but I don't want our shared journey to end!

Kim

I have to say that writing my part of this book is the hardest thing I've ever done. I like to write and writing has been an integral part of my life as well as an instrumental part of my healing journey. But sharing the most intimate details of Dan and my last moments together, admitting the agony, lack of control and state and hopelessness that I found myself in after he died, and transitioning to a life that quite frankly will shock most of my family and friends, seemed a little too transparent for my comfort. Many times, while writing my story, I questioned if I was doing the right thing and even if I was really willing to share the biggest secrets of my life with the world. But no matter how hard I resisted, something always kept pushing me forward. Telling my story to the world was not something I ever envisioned doing. This was truly a labor of love and compassion, for Dan, for the old me who was hopelessly stuck and at times unwilling to surrender, and for the new, more authentic me that I was brave and curious enough to become. I hope that you all find something that you are called to do but that terrifies and challenges you like never before, and the Universe doesn't let you take a pass on. Personal growth doesn't even begin to describe the reluctance, doubt, and eventual expansion and transformation that I have experienced. It wasn't pretty, but I did it. Despite the discomfort, I am eternally grateful for the process, the lessons, and the renewal.

Sarina

I love talking with J.T. He gives it to me straight and I never have to worry about whether what he says is for my highest good. It always is. When he told me we were all going to write a book about our experiences, of course, I thought, "Hasn't that been done…a million times over?" My focus has always been to bring value to my readers and give them something to think about. His reply was, "But it has not been done by the four of you, with our help." Yes, this is absolutely true. He reminds me that each person has a unique view and perspective, and even though there are other books with similar content, the way in which we write this book and share our experiences is unique.

In the beginning, the book had a totally different focus. It was about the wisdom our beautiful loved ones have on the other side, and how that has changed our lives. Our working title of the book included this premise. Somewhere along the way, J.T., Justin, Chase and Dan changed the focus entirely to be about LOVE. After all, it is all about love—what they have done for us and what our loved ones continue to do across the veil.

J.T. says down the line he and I will write the wisdom book, but what the world needs right now is love. We hope you can feel the love in these pages. Thank you for taking this journey with us!

Acknowledgments

There are many people we wish to acknowledge:

Vickie: There is so much gratitude in my heart for so many who have brought me to the completion of this project. A special thank you to dear friends Linda, Shelly and Ann, for lending a listening ear and for the never-ending encouragement, and to Sarina for generously sharing her knowledge and showing me the possibilities. And to everyone that has kept me standing when I was unable to stand on my own, thank you.

Carrie: I would like to thank my daughter, Sadie, who is my hero and the embodiment of perseverance. I am also deeply grateful to my family and friends, all of whom are too numerous to list by name. I am blessed to have you all in my life, so please know you are appreciated and loved. My hometown Allegheny-Clarion Valley community has also supported me immensely and kept me afloat through this journey, and I am deeply grateful to all of you as well.

Kim: I would like to thank my dogs, Butch and Bella, who travelled the road of grief and recovery with me, and participated eagerly in my transformation. I would also like to thank the friends who supported and encouraged me to share what I have learned in this writing adventure.

Sarina: I would like to thank my family, John, Anthony and Z, who have always been my strength and safe place to land. Also, my incredible students, who have taught me so much about who I am and have made me such a better person and teacher. And my dearest friend, Lisa White, for being my sounding board and confidant.

We would also like to acknowledge our incredible editor, Claire Shepherd. Your insight was invaluable! We so appreciate you!

About The Authors

Vickie Hays established a career as a paralegal and law office manager while raising four children and completing her college degree. The sudden loss of her son, Justin, and the events that followed, forced her to question her logic-based thinking that she had developed while working in the legal field. During the days and weeks that followed her son's passing, she discovered that not only was Justin still with her, but that she was able to communicate with him. As Vickie was grieving, she began volunteering for a non-profit horse ranch that provides services to military veterans. It was while volunteering that she was reunited with her childhood friend, the Horse. She was delighted to learn how the unique Horse energy lends an environment for holding space and aids in emotional healing. Vickie, with Justin's guidance, now focuses on healing with horses, and has a special interest in working with the military veteran community. She is a medium and Reiki Master Teacher, currently developing a program to encourage transformation and personal growth through the wisdom of the Horse. Vickie also enjoys reading, gardening, and being in nature. She lives in Northern Michigan near her daughters and their families.

Carrie Hackwelder-Longo has always lived along the shores of the Allegheny River in Western Pennsylvania, bouncing between multiple neighborhoods in Pittsburgh and several rural towns seventy miles north. Originally dreaming of having the life of a metropolitan jetsetter, she has finally come to appreciate the beauty of the hills and valleys, love between small-town neighbors, and the bountiful gifts from the Universe found in the area. Although Carrie currently teaches middle school level English and reading (and loves it), it is her role as a student that is most defining—whether it be immersing herself in poetry and prose, or, more importantly, learning life's lessons from being a human among other humans on this earth.

As a lifelong learner, Carrie has worked for years meditating and preparing to connect with Spirit. She also continues to grow and learn from those who are far more experienced. Using wisdom from loved ones and guides merged with a background in writing, Carrie hopes to share her journey with others. She often chuckles when she recalls her father asking what she would ever do with a degree in English writing… thank goodness Spirit knew all along.

Kim Latta spent 35 years in traditional government and non-profit work providing services to older adults and people with disabilities and coordinating health education programs. But in 2020, after the death of her husband, she quit her government job and began a new path into energy work, communication with animals, and communication with people and animals who have crossed over. Since then, she has become Reiki certified for animals and people, trained in animal communication, and certified to provide Dolphin and Whale Healing Energy services for people and animals. As part of this certification process, many animals have enjoyed the experience of receiving this unique healing energy and all animals have been enthusiastic about offering her their feedback about their healing session. Throughout Kim's transition, her husband, Dan, has been the biggest supporter and often sends messages of encouragement from the other side of the veil. She feels especially passionate about and called to share healing energy with animals and all living things in nature and sees them as partners in the healing process. She offers the healing energy and lets them decide if they want to receive it or not, and for what they want to use the energy. Kim has spent time traveling to other countries to be with dolphins, whales, horses, lions, and other animals in their natural setting to learn about their spiritual gifts and messages for mankind. Kim lives in Longmont, Colorado and through Animals Feel

Better, she provides mobile in-person and distance Reiki services and other energy work to help animals feel better, naturally.

Sarina Baptista is an award-winning author, international speaker, spiritual teacher, and evidential psychic medium. Her book, *My View from Heaven*, is a 2019 COVR Visionary Awards Bronze Recipient in the Iconic Book category, and the 2021 Speak Up Talk Radio Firebird Book Award Winner in three categories. She was a featured speaker for the "Life, Death and Beyond" International Conference in Crete, Greece, and is a visiting medium at Lily Dale, NY, during their summer program. She is a presenter at the IANDS Conferences, and has created many training programs, including spiritual mentoring, workshops, and retreats. Sarina discovered her gifts through her own tragedy—the passing of her seven-year-old son in March 2007. She learned that her son did not really die. He was still very close, and he led her to her incredible gifts.

Sarina's award-winning book, *My View from Heaven: A Boy's Story of His Journey to Heaven and the Purpose of Life on Earth* released December 2014 was written by her son J.T. to answer questions about where he is, how he found his way, what he's doing now and why we choose to come to Earth in the first place. Sarina also has two other books. *A Bridge to Healing: J.T.'s Story — A Mother's Grief Journey and Return to Hope* is about her grief journey and how she found her son again. Her book released in December 2013, *A Bridge to Healing: J.T.'s Story Companion Workbook*, takes the work she has learned from her son to a new level to teach others what they need to know to have clear connection with their angels, guides and loved ones on the other side. J.T. also created an oracle card deck, *The Channeling J.T. Oracle Cards*, to assist people seeking their own answers.

It is Sarina's mission is to help you find purpose and connection to your highest Divine Self, create the bridge for conversation with loved ones who have passed, and mentor psychics and mediums to be master messengers. Sarina currently lives in Melbourne, Florida with her husband, son, two dogs and two cats.

Resources

Below are resources for the reader to explore more about this subject matter and the concepts in this book.

Books

My View from Heaven, by Sarina Baptista (Bridge to Healing Press, 2014)
Power of the Soul, by John Holland (Hay House, 2007)
Many Lives, Many Masters, by Brian L. Weiss, M.D. (Fireside, 1988)
Journey of Souls, by Michael Newton, Ph.D. (Llewellyn, 1994)
What Do You Mean the Third Dimension Is Going Away, by Jim Self (Inner Sight Press, 2013)

Websites

Bridge to Healing – Sarina Baptista
sarinabaptista.com

Animals Feel Better – Kim Latta
animalsfeelbetter.com

Vickie Hays
vickiehays.com

Whale and Dolphin Wisdom Retreats – Anne Gordon
whaleanddolphinwisdomretreats.com

Sacred Acoustics
sacredacoustics.com

www.ingramcontent.com/pod-product-compliance
Lightning Source LLC
Chambersburg PA
CBHW050442010526
44118CB00013B/1637